Crowning Wisdom
An Inspirational Reference Guide

Tracie A. Dawson

Copyright © 2015 Tracie A. Dawson

All rights reserved.

No part of this book may be reproduced in any form or by any electronic or mechanical means including information storage and retrieval systems, without permission in writing from the author. The only exception is by a reviewer, who may quote short excerpts in a review.

Printed by CreateSpace, An Amazon.com Company

2015

To my beloved husband, Matt, and our precious blessings, Parker, Thomas, and Charlotte

Wisdom is supreme; therefore get wisdom. Though it cost all you have, get understanding. Esteem her, and she will exalt you; embrace her, and she will honor you. She will set a garland of grace on your head and present you with a crown of splendor.

Proverbs 4.7-9

Contents

	Foreword	ix
	Prologue	xi
1	Anger: Beating A Car Into Submission	1
	Anger & Self Control	7
	Enemies	8
	Fighting, Arguments & Disputes	8
2	Anxiety: Unwelcome Intruders	10
	Trust	19
	Protection	19
	Fear	19
3	Character: He Gives And Takes Away	21
	Character Development	26
	Loyalty & Trust	30
	Instruction & Discernment	31
	Honor & Humility	31
	Justice	31
	Leadership & Kingship	32
	Patience	32
	Righteous & Upright	33
4	Childrearing: An Oatmeal Shower	35
	To Parents & Children	40

	Discipline & Correction	40
5	**FRIENDSHIP: REINFORCEMENTS HAVE ARRIVED**	43
	Friends, Neighbors, & Random Citizens	49
6	**LIFE: OUTSIDE OF EDEN**	51
	Life	57
	Balance & Moderation	58
	Dissatisfaction	58
	Heart & Spirit	58
	The Home & Homestead	59
	Love	59
	Priorities	59
	Purpose & Duty	59
	Work	60
7	**SOCIAL ISSUES: BREAKING THE CYCLE**	61
	Busybody & Meddler	71
	The Hypocrite	71
	The Mischievous & Troublemaker	71
	Mockers & Scoffers	71
	Thief & Robber	72
	Laziness & The Sluggard	72
	The Unfaithful	73
	Wickedness & Evil	73
8	**TONGUE & SPEECH: A RESTLESS EVIL**	75
	Tongue & Speech	84
	False Testimony & Lies	84

	Gossip	85
	Words of the Wise vs. Speech of Fools	85
9	**WARNING! "CANCEL THE FIRE TRUCKS"**	87
	A Strong Warning Against Adultery	94
	Business & Fraud	96
	Drunkenness	96
	Enticement	97
	Fools & Their Folly	98
	Greed & Envy	100
	Indulgence	100
	Pride	101
	Ruin & Consequences of Deception	101
	The Stingy Man	101
10	**WEALTH & RESOURCES: FRUIT LOOPS & WINE**	103
	Rich Man & Poor Man	109
	Wealth & Resources	110
11	**WISDOM: "THE FOOL DOTH THINK HE IS WISE"**	111
	Knowledge	119
	Wisdom	119
	Solomon's Wisdom One Liners: A Selection	121
12	**WOMEN: MIRACLE BRAS & CHASTITY BELTS**	123
	Feminism Today	125
	Traditionalism Today	127
	To Women	132

Prov 31. 10-31	135
APPENDIX	137
ACKNOWLEDGEMENTS	149
ABOUT THE AUTHOR	151
ENDNOTES	152

Foreword

When I first began this project, it was for my own personal use. Intent on learning what the Bible says about discipline and how to teach my children, I earnestly sought God's directives regarding how to *train up a child in the way he should go* but needed a Scriptural foundation for how that might be accomplished.

As I began to study the Proverbs, I found an abundance of Scripture speaking specifically to childrearing and also a wealth of guidelines for walking in wisdom, living a God-honoring life, preserving integrity, and avoiding the pitfalls of foolishness.

In Scriptures, the blessings of wisdom are often described as a crown. Today, a crown can also depict the summit of a mountain, a pinnacle, or the culmination of one's research, work, or knowledge. This is where the title, Crowning Wisdom, is derived. Not only does the student of wisdom gain benefits of applied wisdom, but he is also honored and elevated as a result of wisdom at work in his life!

However, I found the Proverbs to be somewhat disordered—it was difficult to locate specific passages as the assemblage resembled more of a collage and less of a collection. So, with subject dividers and simple loose-leaf notebook paper, I began to organize the Proverbs according to my own understanding of their meaning and subject matter. This is not an exhaustive concordance of the Proverbs, but rather, a quick-reference guide to major topics and themes within the Proverbs and a sampling of the verses that have made the greatest impact on me.

Most verses will be from The Holy Bible, New International Version, Grand Rapids, Michigan (Zondervan) 1973, 1978, 1984 unless otherwise indicated by the footnote number one. All Scripture taken from The Holy Bible (NIV) are within fair use guidelines to the best of our interpretation of those guidelines and limitations.

To introduce each chapter, I have shared some of my own anecdotes, struggles, and revelations, as well as those from friends kind enough to share their own. My personal accounts are examples primarily of what not to do, further substantiating my need for a book such as this.

I actually wrote this book for me.

This personal guide to the Proverbs has been a passion of mine and hopefully will be a source of information, encouragement, and instruction to any reader.

Although we cannot expect every Proverb to be fully expressed in our fallen world, nor can we claim each one as a literal promise, we can become students of Wisdom and grow in knowledge, character, and honor. We can have a fuller understanding of the nature of God, the author of truth and wisdom, and believe that in light of eternity, His Word, purposes, and truth will ultimately prevail.

I encourage you to take your time with this book. Allow each chapter and its challenge to greater wisdom to speak to your heart as you listen and become wiser. I hope it will be something you can turn to when you need wisdom, understanding, and peace. My prayer is that this book will bless you as you yourself embrace the Wisdom that graces your head and presents you with a crown of splendor!

Prologue

Solomon, author of most of the Proverbs, discerned that he lacked wisdom and was unequal to the task of leading the great nation of Israel. We, too, often recognize our need for godly wisdom in life. However, today our search for wisdom and understanding begins with our friends, self-help books, counseling, conferences, and classes. Rarely do we consult the actual book on wisdom, nor do we realize the necessary foundation for this insight we seek.

The wisdom Solomon had was divine—a gift from God in response to his humble request and reverence for the God of his father, David.

Prov 1.1-7 explains the purpose and benefits of wisdom, while reminding us that, first and foremost, our foundation for this knowledge must be a proper respect and reverence for God Himself.

> *These are the proverbs of Solomon, David's son, king of Israel. Their purpose is to teach people wisdom and discipline, to help them understand the insights of the wise. Their purpose is to teach people to live disciplined and successful lives, to help them do what is right, just, and fair. These proverbs will give insight to the simple, knowledge and discernment to the young. Let the wise listen to these proverbs and become even wiser. Let those with understanding receive guidance by exploring the meaning in these proverbs and parables, the words of the wise and their riddles. Fear of the LORD is the foundation of true knowledge, but fools despise wisdom and discipline.*[1]

Nearly a thousand years later, Jesus had a conversation with his followers about His use of analogies and illustrations. They were called parables and were somewhat ambiguous to his audience. Interpretation and application of His parables also required a foundation—acceptance of Christ and His Messianic mission. Without that, His stories were confusing and senseless. But when built on the proper foundation, they revealed truth and knowledge which increased their wisdom. *He replied, "The knowledge of the secrets of the kingdom of heaven has been given to you, but not to them. Whoever has will be given more, and he will have an abundance. Whoever does not have, even what he has will be taken from him."* Matthew 13.11-12

The passage above assures the Christ-follower that knowledge of the truth has been given to us and will increase in abundance.

My prayer for you is that God will open the eyes of your heart and increase your wisdom so that you will have it in abundance. Ask Him for discernment and understanding. James 1.5 assures us *If any of you lack wisdom, he should ask God, who gives generously to all without finding fault, and it will be given to him.*

May God bless you abundantly on your journey to greater knowledge, insight, and Crowning Wisdom!

Chapter One

ANGER: BEATING A CAR INTO SUBMISSION

We all have probably witnessed the toddler in the store, fighting and flailing after a parent refuses to buy something the child wants. We might not throw temper tantrums like a youngster, but most of us experience varying degrees of anger throughout the week and even each day. How about the driver who cuts you off in traffic or the store clerk who is unable or simply unwilling to provide the service you need? What about the co-worker or boss who takes credit for your work? Maybe it is a spouse or friend who has betrayed you?

*****

Remove the dross from the silver, and out comes material for the silversmith. Prov 25.4

My husband and I had been married eight years, yet I had only seen him truly angry twice. I am referring to anger that makes the blood boil, the face flush, the heart pound, and the eyes wild and crazy. If you knew my husband, you would probably laugh at the absurdity of him ever reaching this state.

Physically speaking, he is extra-large, extra tall, and extra LOUD, BUT, he is gracious, kindhearted, and very patient. Most of our friends lovingly refer to him as a jolly gentle giant. Little did we know that he, like all of us, needed spiritual refining.

It began late one night after dinner. The car we owned at the time occasionally refused to start, making traveling quite stressful. Generally, automobile problems were common for us as we usually bought used cars with fairly high mileage.

We had taken it to a number of mechanics, to no avail. They could not isolate the problem or replicate it; therefore, they could not fix it. For months we drove this car that randomly and inexplicably refused to start. Oftentimes, it would simply require us to wait for 15 minutes to an hour or so, and then it would start right up.

On this particular evening, we finished a late supper with friends and said our goodbyes as the restaurant closed. The streets were empty as we set out for the long drive home. But our fickle car refused to start.

At first, I howled in laughter at the ridiculous timing. The problem, however, was that my gracious and kindhearted husband was finally out of patience.

He popped the hood for the obligatory inspection of the car's engine. (We had done this before and knew that it was fruitless, but it was the instinctual thing to do.) Next, we looked in the trunk for something. Anything. Suspicious that this was the result of an electrical short, we thought that if we could wiggle a wire or "jar" the system, maybe the connection would be restored.

Being neither mechanically-inclined nor prepared for the unexpected, there were no tools in the trunk for such an experiment. My small 5-pound dumbbells (for exercising on the go, I guess?), a beach towel, and a few other random items summed up the entire contents of the trunk.

*****

A fool gives full vent to his anger, but a wise man keeps himself under control. Prov 29.11

You've probably heard the saying "desperate times call for desperate measures." My husband was desperate to start the car, which brings me to one of the most humorous and humiliating memories we share.

Comically, my husband chose one of the 5-pound dumbbells as the instrument for his "experiment." He walked around to the exposed engine and proceeded to unleash on it the fury of a man at his wits' end.

The sights and sounds are seared into my memory—the echo of clanking metal on metal reverberated through the empty streets. I cringed at the sound, imagining the entire engine dropping through the chassis and plunking down on the pavement. Surprisingly, the car still did not start after such thrashing!

I didn't really know what part of the engine he physically struck, but I just knew at that point, it was between him and the car, and I needed to stay out of it.

Of course, I begged him to stop, which he did...eventually. Next, he threw the small barbell back into the trunk, slammed the lid, seated himself in the car, and locked the doors...leaving me out in the cold. I don't know what actually happened in the car at that moment, but there was shouting, rustling, and a lot of banging on the steering wheel.

He would not speak to me nor acknowledge my protests. He was exasperated. The fire had been ignited and the silver began yielding to the power of the heat. But would the silver give up its dross?

My initial amusement at the situation turned to pity as I witnessed the undoing of my sweet and gentle husband.

Once I realized that this electrical short was not going to make the connection, I pulled out my new flip phone and called an aunt, who lived nearby. She picked us up and loaned us her car to drive home. We left our car parked on the street and made our way home in silence.

The next morning, my husband towed the car to a mechanic, fully anticipating that at this point the mechanic must be able to pinpoint the malfunction and repair it. However, as he arrived at the mechanic's shop, the car cranked immediately and the engine purred. You gotta be kidding me!

Had he not been in the presence of strangers, he would have probably retrieved the barbell and begun round two, with even greater fury!

*****

Many are the plans in a man's heart, but it is the LORD's purpose that prevails. Prov 19.21

When we share this story with friends, of course, we laugh hysterically at the absurdity of that night and my husband's ludicrous efforts at beating the car into submission. But he also admits that it was one of the darkest moments in his heart and soul, where he went to a place filled with hatred and fury and emerged feeling weak and totally defeated.

Our response to adversity is an indicator of spiritual maturity and purity. Due to the fall of man into sin, our nature is corrupt: prideful, impatient, and demanding. We struggle when things do not go our way or within our timing.

Yet, we are not without value. The Master Craftsman sees the beauty and glory of what could be, in spite of what is. He has a purpose and plan for each person and is committed to crafting each one of us into a glorious work of art.

My dear husband began as the raw material for the silversmith, filled with impurities that needed to be drawn out. The process was painful and embarrassing as he clearly resisted, but God is patient with His children, He knows our worth and potential, and He never quits working. He takes the ordinary, and creates something extraordinary.

We all have dross in our lives. It may manifest itself in anger, pride, lust, greed, idolatry, or anything that points back to self. Yet the difficulty in how dross is removed from our lives depends entirely on us!

We can resist and rebel, refusing to yield and give up what has tainted our hearts, or we can surrender our impurities and trust in the merciful hands of the Master Craftsman.

Once purged of the impurities, He restores and redeems. He begins to bend and stretch us, deliberately impressing His character into our hearts, shaping us into something rare and exquisite. We are changed for the better. We no longer exist as before, but now are transformed into a new creation possessing greater depth, beauty, and purpose.

*****

A patient man has great understanding, but a quick-tempered man displays folly. Prov 14.29

Eventually, the electrical short was identified and the car repaired. We gave the matter over to God and acknowledged that we were not in control but that He could resolve this when He chose. We no longer stressed over the reliability of that vehicle, as God was always faithful to provide alternative transportation as we needed.

Over time, the spiritual transformation in the heart of my husband became apparent. He is grateful today for that experience as he has a deeper understanding and compassion for those struggling with the darkness in their own hearts, with feelings of rage and insufficiency, and with our universal need for a Savior.

He is more patient and understanding with those around him and no longer impulsive when adversity comes. It was both humbling and enlightening for him to undergo such refining, yet the end justified the means.

This season in our lives was purposeful and beneficial—Matt recognized his own weakness and the inevitable defeat in succumbing to his anger. But after repenting of his behavior and recognizing the unhealthy condition of his heart, he sought wisdom and trusted in God's provision and sovereignty.

It took time, discipline, self-examination, and the Holy Spirit at work within him. As he listened and obeyed, the filth and scum were skimmed away. The dross could be removed and the silver made pure.

We all face circumstances that vary in degrees of severity and consequence. Fortunately, this light-hearted example illustrates how even the most insignificant mishaps can drive us to foolishness and a loss of control. But maybe yours isn't so humorous.

Maybe you have hurt others with your words and actions. If so, we are simply to stop and seek forgiveness from those we have hurt and from God whom we've sinned against. He will forgive and restore. I John 1.9 states, *If we confess our sin, He is faithful and just and will forgive us our sins and purify us from all unrighteousness.*

He will draw out the impurities and begin crafting us into a glorious work of art.

*****

Crowning Wisdom

Proverbs has stern warnings about uncontrolled anger, conflict, and vengeance, as their products are strife, foolishness, and ruin.

When we succumb to anger and rage, we choose a descending path that ultimately leads to defeat. We resist God's revelation of those pollutants in our hearts and minds, potentially sabotaging our own blessings and the future plans He has for us.

However, if we recognize that victory is possible, that the Master Craftsman can purify and transform each and every one of us into something rare and exquisite, we choose the path that elevates us to wisdom that crowns.

Proverbs encourages those who strive to exercise patience, control, and restraint; they are blessed with understanding, wisdom, and honor. It is the path that expands the view of ourselves and others. We see beyond the moment and trust in His ability to right the wrongs and to redeem each and every circumstance we will face. Then we are free to experience the *Blessings [that] crown the head of the righteous...* Prov 10.6a

ANGER & SELF CONTROL

- Prov 14.29 *People with understanding control their anger; a hot temper shows great foolishness.*[1]

- Prov 16.32 *Better to be patient than powerful; better to have self-control than to conquer a city.*[1]

- Prov 22.24-25 *Do not make friends with a hot-tempered man, do not associate with one easily angered, or you may learn his ways and get yourself ensnared.*

- Prov 20.22 *Do not say, "I'll pay you back for this wrong!" Wait for the Lord and He will deliver you.*

ENEMIES

- Prov 25.21-22 *If your enemy is hungry, give him food to eat; if he is thirsty, give him water to drink. In doing this, you will heap burning coals on his head, and the Lord will reward you.*

- Prov 26.27 *Whoever digs a pit will fall into it, and a stone will come back on him who starts it rolling.*[1]

FIGHTING, ARGUMENTS & DISPUTES

- Prov 29.8 *Mockers stir up a city, but wise men turn away anger.*

    *Mockers or scoffers are those who ultimately reject any form of wisdom and instruction. Webster's Dictionary defines a mocker as one who attacks and ridicules others, defies authority, deceives, jeers, and imitates. They taunt, tease, and mislead others. Not only do they reject instruction, but they ridicule the instructor and others in search of greater wisdom.

- Prov 17.1 *Better a dry crust eaten in peace than a house filled with feasting—and conflict.*[1]

- Prov 17.14 *Starting a quarrel is like breaching a dam; so drop the matter before a dispute breaks out.*

Chapter Two

ANXIETY: UNWELCOME INTRUDERS

"Your body is rejecting your life."
–My husband, 2011

I come from a long line of worriers. My great grandmother used to worry that the woman "in the television box" was flirting with her husband when television personality Betty Feezor cooked magnificent meals, then held them out for viewers to admire. She went around the home fussing and fretting that this woman was trying to lure her husband away from her.

Okay, I admit, she was a bit nuts. This was after dementia had set in and she was an invalid living with her son and daughter-in-law. I grew up hearing stories of their obvious confusion over the characters on television.

But there's also my grandmother who lived through the Great Depression. That era left an indelible mark on her entire generation. She agonized over food supplies and never let anything go to waste. I remember her scolding me for carelessly peeling an apple and taking too much of the pulp off with the skin.

She had known a hunger and poverty most of us will never, ever understand. This drove her to hoard things later in life: newspapers, magazines, books, clothes, fabric, furniture, and all kinds of useless stuff. She feared there may be another economic collapse and tried to avoid disaster by retaining everything and preparing for the worst.

My mother worries too. She doesn't mean to. She knows it's unhealthy and unproductive, but she worries nevertheless. This is evident through the frequent inquiries about the wellbeing and condition of our children, the church my husband pastors, and pretty much every aspect of our lives.

But I probably take the cake. It began when I was young. I had a dream...a nightmare actually. I dreamt I had been kidnapped. No one could help me, no one could find me, and I had nothing to help me survive. It was distressing: the kind of nightmare where you wake up soaked in sweat, heart racing, and totally disoriented.

It bothered me for days. I couldn't shake the feeling of impending doom. I talked to my parents, but they dismissed my concerns, "It was just a bad dream. We all have them from time to time."

Yet I worried that it must be a warning of actual danger ahead. Didn't God speak to lots of Biblical characters through their dreams? Joseph was warned in a dream to flee to Egypt with Mary and baby Jesus. Maybe my dream was a warning too!

So what did I do?

I packed a bag. I prepared for an actual kidnapping and thought through all of the supplies I would need to cope.

I packed my toothbrush and toothpaste (scarred by my first dental fillings made an oral hygiene believer out of me), a comb, brush, a change of clothing and underwear, and then snacks.

I carried the bag around and had it at the ready, should the moment come when I least expected it. I was a little embarrassed to admit to others why I lugged this bag with me wherever I went, but it gave me comfort to know that I would be prepared with my necessities, worst case scenario.

Then it occurred to me—one day those provisions would be exhausted and I would be left struggling to survive anyway.

That too made me anxious.

The apostle Paul said that we can boast in our weaknesses, so I'll just go ahead and admit it, I'm a pretty spectacular worrywart. I'm excellent at it...possibly the best in the world. In fact, if worrying were an Olympic sport, I would be a gold medalist several times over.

I am the Michael Phelps of worrying.

*****

Having a bent towards order and control, a high-strung person like me struggles with the realization that I actually control nothing—that God alone brings order to my chaotic world. I recognized it as a child and still fight it as an adult.

I am powerless to elicit the changes that bring me relief from that painful stretching of my mind, body, and soul which wears me down to the point of indecision, exhaustion, and ultimately to despair.

The trouble with anxiety is that its root lies in a great deception. We have been deceived into thinking that if we discipline and control our lives (i.e. our circumstances, relationships, even our sinful hearts), then we can "manage" life and even find it fulfilling at times. Our entire position in life is defensive. Protection and prevention becomes paramount in our anxiety-driven efforts to control situations, other people, and even our futures.

My grandmother tried to control her future by preparing for another depression. I prepared for my kidnapping by packing a bag.

Yet Scripture tells us that some things are unavoidable. We will face adversity: Christ followers will often be rejected by the world, there will be times of temptation and trials, and God allows rain to fall on the just and the unjust.[2] We must admit, these things we certainly cannot predict or control.

I wish I could tell you that I have spiritually outgrown anxiety, that I am now laid back, easy-going, and walk in complete confidence in all situations, but in all honesty, it is a battle that I continue to fight.

In fact, the last few years have been rather difficult on our family emotionally, financially, and spiritually. We experienced our second miscarriage, the tragic loss of a young relative, the loss of a dear aunt to cancer, coupled with a new pastorate of a very fragile church, struggles in homeschooling, and my daughter's first infestation with lice.

Embarrassingly, the issue that sent me over the edge was the lice!

I can exercise my spiritual "muscles" over financial issues. Paul gives us a great example in Philippians 4.12,13, *I have learned the secret of being content in any and every situation...I can do everything through Him who gives me strength.*

I also found countless comforts in Scripture to help me continue to trust God in spite of pregnancy loss and family tragedy, for He has brought peace and comfort that transcends our understanding.[3]

He joyfully sustained us through difficult transitions in ministry as well as the challenges in home education. Like the

Psalmist in 94.19, *When anxiety was great within me, your consolation brought joy to my soul.*

However, I did not know how to wrestle through the issue of lice. I had no frame of reference or Biblical example for this kind of challenge, silly as it sounds.

I was humiliated and left cowering in fear—fear of judgment from others and fear of a foe I neither understood nor could control. It left me doubled over, gasping for air.

I panicked and went into overdrive. I could not eat, could not sleep, could not visit friends, and certainly could not have anyone into my home! I wanted to tent the house and drop a de-louse A-bomb while diving out of a window! But you can't blow up your kid's head! That's probably frowned upon.

Then I considered shaving her hair...all 18 inches!

So I declared all-out war on lice and was willing to pay any price for victory. There would be no eating, sleeping, relaxing, or fun in my home until these pests were annihilated!

Then my body began to respond to this madness. I had headaches, sleep disturbances, imaginations of bugs in my own hair, and violent mood swings. Perplexed(honestly), I asked my husband one day, "What is wrong with me?" He retorted, "Your body is rejecting your life!"

I couldn't help but laugh at the absurd truth of his statement.

*****

Many Scriptures address anxiety and worry. I Peter 5.7 urges us to *Cast all your anxiety on Him because He cares for you,* and Philippians 4.6-7 reiterates:

Do not be anxious about anything, but in everything, by prayer and petition, with thanksgiving, present your requests to God. And the peace of God, which transcends all understanding, will guard your hearts and your minds in Christ Jesus.

Of course, there are varying degrees of anxiety. I do not want to minimize and disregard the many issues and medical conditions which drive clinical forms of anxiety, such as a chemical imbalance, physical trauma, things rooted in painful past experiences, unhealthy relationships, or holding on to guilt for past mistakes.

Professional Christian counseling or medical treatment may be necessary and beneficial in those cases, but I also believe that God's Word (which is *living and active*[4]) offers comfort and guidance to even extreme presentations of anxiety.

But it requires us to do something I had not done before.

*****

We all need that transcendent peace that Paul described in Philippians, but I could not get there. I could not stop being anxious; I could not *cast it* on Him and fully let go of it. I didn't trust that this issue would be as important to God as it was to me, so I refused to let go of it. I became weighed down and tormented by things beyond my understanding and control.

Sure, I prayed (actually pleaded) with God to help us eradicate these unwelcome intruders, but I remained anxious and took the offensive to such a degree that it wreaked havoc on my body and our entire family.

I was foolishly trying to regulate the situation and resolve it in my own timing.

However, He tells us in Ecclesiastes 11.10a, *Banish anxiety from your heart, cast off the troubles of your body,* and again in Psalm 55.22, *Cast your cares on the Lord and He will sustain you.*

If we continue to hold on to the anxiety and the circumstances that drive it, giving them our thoughts, energy, and attention, we have not actually obeyed Scripture.

He urges us to banish it from our hearts, to cast it upon Him (withdraw from it, lay it down and walk away), and then He will sustain (guide, feed, hold, be present with) us in the midst of it.

When we think we must hold on to worries, sorrow, and anxiety because they are important issues that affect our lives, He still tells us to give them over to Him. Put them down and walk away.

Yet, I admit, it is hard to simply eliminate behaviors or negative thought patterns and practices. Even Dr. Phil will tell you that much! They leave a void which once created, longs to be filled with something.

Smokers don't often effectively quit smoking cold turkey, they must replace the habit of smoking with chewing gum, eating celery sticks, or massive quantities of chocolate—something to replace that satisfaction gained from the very act of smoking.

Likewise, when we simply eliminate anxious thoughts and behaviors, we may feel something is missing: like a city with a broken wall—weakened by the holes and cracks created when pieces are removed or destroyed. We are often left feeling incomplete and vulnerable to possibly worse intruders.

What we must attempt to do is fill those voids with structurally sound reinforcements. Paul also knew this was the only way to combat our anxiety.

He stressed the importance of prayer, thanksgiving, and simply taking our petitions to God. That's the *casting it on Him* part described in Philippians 4.6-7, but he goes on further in verse 8 giving practical advice for how to repair walls that have been weakened by removing those anxious thoughts: *Fix your thoughts on what is true, and honorable, and right, and pure, and lovely, and admirable. Think about things that are excellent and worthy of praise.*[1]

Those are the exact opposite of anxious thoughts!

Of course, this doesn't mean we don't face the issues. We still must pay our debts, we still must address unhealthiness in our relationships, we must still take responsibility for our actions, but when we prayerfully cast our cares on Him, with gratitude for the good things already granted in Christ—a precursor to the positive thinking he describes in verse 8, He brings us peace that transcends our immediate circumstances.

His peace guards our hearts and minds in Christ Jesus, acting as sentinel around the mended walls of our city.

*****

*For the despondent, every day brings trouble; for
the happy heart, life is a continual feast.*
Prov 15.15

We are then free to rebuild the wall with healthy thoughts, brought on by a thankful heart, uplifted by His faithfulness, not a despondent and heavy heart, weighed down by anxiety. We begin to fill those gaps with materials stronger, more enduring, and without limit, which is the continual feast of the happy heart.

When we trust things will be accomplished according to His perfect will, we no longer agonize over having everything accomplished according to our own.

Then comes His presence and provision. He will care for us. He will sustain us.

*****

Crowning Wisdom

Proverbs 12.25 states that *An anxious heart weighs a man down, but a kind word cheers him up*. An anxious heart is a heart carrying a load it was not designed to bear. When we attempt to control everything, especially the future, we may eventually recognize our futility and foolishness because it is a trust in self.

He is trustworthy and offers protection for those who are discerning and walk with integrity. He is a refuge, a fortress, assuring us protection as we go on our way, as we encounter rough roads ahead, and even when we are at our most vulnerable—as we rest.

My prayer is for those of us who battle heavy hearts brought on by things great and small, that we can truly cast our cares on Him, trusting Him, and *resting content, untouched by trouble.*

Trust

- Prov 28.26 *He who trusts in himself is a fool, but he who walks in wisdom is kept safe.*

- Prov 3.5-6 *Trust in the Lord with all your heart, and lean not on your own understanding; in all your ways acknowledge him and he will make your path straight.*

Protection

- Prov 2.7-8 *He grants a treasure of common sense to the honest. He is a shield to those who walk with integrity. He guards the paths of the just and protects those who are faithful to him.*[1]

- Prov 3.21-26 *My child, don't lose sight of common sense and discernment. Hang on to them, for they will refresh your soul. They are like jewels on a necklace. They keep you safe on your way, and your feet will not stumble. You can go to bed without fear; you will lie down and sleep soundly. You need not be afraid of sudden disaster or the destruction that comes upon the wicked, for the Lord is your security. He will keep your foot from being caught in a trap.*[1]

- Prov 21.30 *No human wisdom or understanding or plan can stand against the Lord.*[1]

- Prov 30.5 *Every word of God is flawless; he is a shield to those who take refuge in Him.*

Fear

- Prov 29.25 *Fear of man will prove to be a snare, but whoever trusts the Lord is kept safe.*

- Prov 19.23 *The fear of the Lord leads to life; Then one rests content, untouched by trouble.*

Chapter Three

CHARACTER: HE GIVES AND TAKES AWAY

> "Character is like a tree and reputation its shadow. The shadow is what we think it is and the tree is the real thing."
> —Abraham Lincoln

We have friends (I will call them John and Meredith) whom we have known for many, many years. My husband and I first met them when we were in the early years of marriage, before children and mortgages, serving in fledgling ministries, and eager for what God had in store for our respective futures.

Although we live in different cities now, we remain close friends, bound by the kinship forged when our lives intersected. It was a precious time when our faithwalks grew and God began a process of testing, trying, and sifting.

I would love to tell you their story in its entirety, but that deserves more detail than can be expressed here. What I do want to share is their painful struggle with infertility for more than 10 years.

Countless doctors, tests, procedures, and treatments convinced John and Meredith that they would never conceive. This was devastating news as both came from large, happy, thriving families and desired the same experience through parenting.

Meredith in particular struggled, especially in the Church, where she perceived an emphasis and celebration of the role of women in bearing children. It was difficult to understand how to serve (in fulltime ministry no less) and honor the God they knew and understood to be all-powerful, capable of absolutely anything, but who had seemingly denied them children.

As their prayers for a family continued, God directed their hearts to adoption. The Bible tells us in Ephesians 1.5 that we, as believers in Christ, are *adopted as his sons in Jesus Christ*. They felt that God had planned for them a family that would depict to the world the immense love He extends to each of us.

However, adoption was not without difficulties. John and Meredith experienced six or more failed adoption attempts, one due to the tragic death of both mother and the unborn child in an automobile crash.

The adoption process was heartbreaking and emotionally draining. It was difficult to accept infertility coupled with seemingly constant setbacks, but they continued to trust God and wait on Him.

*****

Then, one day, John was told by their adoption agency that they had been selected by a birth mother and that she was not having one baby, but twins! After many painful failed adoption attempts, John was cautious and protective of Meredith's heart. He did not share the news of this with her until the adoption was certain.

Imagine her joy when she learned that not only was she preparing to pick up her adoptive son but that she must prepare for his twin brother too! She had often dreamt of having twins! We rejoiced with them and praised God for His answer to all our prayers.

A year or two later, John and Meredith adopted another boy. Then another. Their home teemed with activity and their hearts overflowed with acceptance, love, and joy at all God had done.

Then God set their sights internationally. Two little boys in an Ethiopian orphanage needed a family. The adoption process moved quickly, and then God did something unexpected.

Meredith became pregnant!

Anyone familiar with fertility and reproductive health can attest that any pregnancy is miraculous as it is a very complicated and fragile process. The significance of this unexpected pregnancy was not lost on anyone! We all marveled and praised God for this additional blessing!

It was exciting and a little overwhelming to plan for three new children, but John and Meredith began to exercise a new level of faith and confidence in God. They knew He could provide for their expanding family, even beyond their anticipated needs.

*****

Meredith progressed through the first trimester beautifully, and at the 18-week checkup, John and Meredith learned they would have a precious little girl. Overwhelmed with joy and awed by God's unfolding plan, they prepared for their upcoming international adoption and the follow-up arrival of their first daughter!

With four boys at home and Meredith pregnant, John and his mother-in-law prepared for the week-long trip to Ethiopia for finalization of the international adoption.

Three days before their departure, Meredith detected something troubling and visited her obstetrician. For reasons unclear at the time, their daughter had perished in utero at 22 weeks. They were devastated.

Meredith and John faced a grim reality. The labor she must endure would not yield the cherished first cry of a newborn—only silence and stillness.

A friend of mine, a former labor and delivery nurse, once shared with me that when a child is born, there is a moment—a pause when everyone in the delivery room seems to hold their breath and wait. Time slows and seconds feel like an eternity. She described it as a very spiritual experience, waiting for the first sign that an infant will fight for life independent of mother. They wait for the first inhaled breath and exhaled protests.

However, for John and Meredith, there was no such pause, no expectant breath of life, only a somber room, reverent with the sadness of life seized from their grasp.

Meredith still felt the pain of labor. She still had to push. She had to birth her beloved daughter. She alone faced the task of bringing her daughter into the world that she would never experience.

It was a lonely and bitter road. Instead of tears of joy, they shed tears of sorrow. Instead of hope, they felt despair. Instead of embracing life, they embraced death.

Words cannot express the darkness and grief that enveloped them. This was not the God they knew. This didn't reflect Him. He wouldn't do something like this. It felt unimaginably cruel!

The day after delivery, they dressed their tiny, yet perfectly formed daughter in a delicate handmade dress and privately said their final goodbyes. Tearfully and prayerfully, they committed to the Lord what was already His and trusted that they would one day meet their daughter, in health and beauty, full of life and joy, in heaven.

The following day, John and his mother-in-law somberly boarded the plane to Ethiopia.

*****

A few years later, a physician discovered an anomaly in Meredith's blood that explained why her pregnancy unexpectedly terminated. This had remained undetected all her life and would have been treatable, had the obstetricians known about it.

This revelation brought both sadness and relief. It was disheartening to learn that this abnormality could have been treated during the pregnancy and that treatment could have saved the life of their daughter. Yet it also brought relief to Meredith, who like other mothers dealing with grief in pregnancy loss, questioned if she had inadvertently done something wrong.

Personally, I struggle to understand why this couple would need to endure such a blow after finally coming to acceptance and peace after years of infertility.

But as Job humbly responded to his own devastating loss, *The Lord gave and the Lord has taken away; may the name of the Lord be praised.*[5] John and Meredith also continue to praise and serve God in His giving and taking away.

*****

I weep in writing this story remembering the hurt and disappointment of friends so very dear to us. I was troubled over praying for a miraculous pregnancy for my friends—a prayer that was answered, but ultimately brought about greater pain and loss.

We have witnessed firsthand their struggle with faith and trust in a God whose ways are higher than our ways and whose thoughts are higher than our thoughts.[6]

We all still ask why? We can't reconcile the point of any of it. And quite possibly, if God did try to explain His way, His plan behind this, we probably could not fully appreciate it.

Ecclesiastes 8.17 explains it this way: *I realized that no one can discover everything God is doing under the sun. Not even the wisest people discover (comprehend) everything, no matter what they claim.*[1]

We simply hope that someday all tears will be wiped away, there will be no more goodbyes, no more sickness or pain, but instead joy and life everlasting.

CHARACTER DEVELOPMENT

I share their story as a powerful example of character. Godly character is developed only after everything else is stripped away. When our strength falls short, when our resources run out, when our connections, influence, or health fails, when control is taken from us, and even when others abuse us, we can know that God uses those circumstances to test our character.

When we survey the faithful men and women of God whose stories are told in Scripture like Job, Abraham, Joseph, Moses, Gideon, Samson, Naomi, David, Esther, we see that all experienced periods of great suffering and testing. As a result, all brought great hope to those around them.

We too must be tested. It is the developmental process by which God brings us through a place of suffering to eventual hope and eternal healing.

Paul explained to the Christians in Rome, *We know that suffering produces perseverance; perseverance, character; and character, hope.*[7]

John and Meredith persevered in their suffering. They continued to trust in a sovereign God whom they knew personally. They recognized that their dreams of a large family were inspired by Him and would be fulfilled by Him in His own way and in His own time!

Years of infertility and heartache have tested and developed their character, but instead of yielding to bitterness and despair, it has produced compassion and hope. Paul's words to the Romans continue, *And hope does not disappoint us, because God has poured out his love into our hearts by the Holy Spirit, whom he has given us.*[8]

Their hope is found in the love of God poured into their lives through the Holy Spirit, who is their counselor and comforter. Sure, they still struggle with sorrow. Their arms still ache to hold their daughter. They still question "Why?" But, they also experience inexplicable joy in raising their six spirited boys.

They are filled with hope and now share that same hope with others facing the same difficult trials they endured. Here is what John and Meredith say about their experience:

> The joy of adoption did not take away the pain of infertility, nor did the pain of infertility diminish our

joy in adopting. We often tell our adoption story and stress that we did not care how children came into our home, only that they came! As time passes, we look back and understand at least some of why God has us adopting; we have couples in our home every month who are dealing with infertility and thinking about adoption. I am a pastor and have received hundreds of emails, letters, texts, and phone calls expressing thanks for sharing our journey. We understand more fully 2 Corinthians 1.3-5, when Paul praised God for the opportunity to give to others the same comfort he had received from God. We love doing that!

The bottom line is that God, in his infinite wisdom, has placed a call on us to adopt. I don't know if we would have ever seen the beauty of it had he not directed our path.

*****

> *When the storm has swept by, the wicked are gone, but the righteous stand firm forever.*
> Prov 10.25

We must expect storms in life. There is no getting around it. Jesus told the story of a foolish man who built his house on sand and a wise man who built his house on a firm foundation. Both faced storms. The only difference was in their foundation.

The foolish man heard Jesus' words but did not put them in practice. Consequently, when the deluge began and the winds battered the home, it fell with a great crash.

The wise man, on the other hand, heard Jesus' words, put them in practice, and as a result, his home remained intact.

Both faced storms, but only one house endured.

The apostle Paul refers to Christ as *the power of God and the wisdom of God.*[9] True wisdom comes from God through his Son, Jesus Christ.

It was through knowing Him that John and Meredith could withstand the torrents of their struggle with infertility. Their confidence in Christ's sovereignty gave them perseverance as they wrestled through lengthy and difficult adoption processes. And their trust in His love and strength saw them through the tempest, the devastating loss of their daughter.

Christ is their foundation. They hear Him and obey. Their home stands firm still today.

*****

Crowning Wisdom

By wisdom a house is built, and through understanding it is established; through knowledge its rooms are filled with rare and beautiful treasure. Prov 24.3-4

When we rely on anything other than Christ, we foolishly build a hut: weak, vulnerable, and resting on shifting sand. It is unprepared for and lacks the strength to withstand the inevitable storms of life.

However, the storms and the sufferings brought on in life are not without value. They serve as opportunities for God to not only reveal the integrity of our foundation but also to develop within us godly character and ultimately a greater hope!

If we rely on Christ and His word to guide and strengthen us, we are building our house, our life, on the bedrock of wisdom. Through understanding, it is established and made secure—reinforced by the Cornerstone, Christ, our source of all wisdom.

We have then built an actual fortress, strong and established, filled with rare and beautiful treasures, resting secure on a foundation impervious to the storms.

The Proverbs address many aspects of character and how they impact our lives and relationships. Please see the note after this selection for further guidance in finding Proverbs for additional character issues.

LOYALTY & TRUST

- Prov 3.3-4 *Never let loyalty and kindness leave you! Tie them around your neck as a reminder. Write them deep within your heart. Then you will find favor with both God and people, and you will earn a good reputation.*[1]

- Prov 28.10 *Those who lead good people along an evil path will fall into their own trap, but the honest will inherit good things.*[1]

- Prov 31.10-12 *A wife of noble character who can find? She is worth far more than rubies. Her husband has full confidence in her and lacks nothing of value. She brings him good, not harm, all the days of her life.*

INSTRUCTION & DISCERNMENT

- Prov 28.11 *A rich man may be wise in his own eyes, but a poor man who has discernment sees through him.*

- Prov 31.26 *She [the wife of noble character] speaks with wisdom, and faithful instruction is on her tongue.*

HONOR & HUMILITY

- Prov 21.21 *He who pursues righteousness and love, finds life, prosperity, and honor.*

- Prov 27.1 *Do not boast about tomorrow, for you do not know what a day may bring forth.*

- Prov 27.2 *Let another praise you, and not your own mouth; someone else, and not your own lips.*

- Prov 29.23 *Pride ends in humiliation, while humility brings honor.*[1]

JUSTICE

- Prov 17.23 *A wicked man accepts a bribe in secret to pervert the course of justice.*

- Prov 18.5 *It is not good to be partial to the wicked or to deprive the innocent of justice.*

- Prov 20.23 *The Lord detests double standards; he is not pleased by dishonest scales.*[1]

- Prov 21.15 *When justice is done, it brings joy to the righteous but terror to evildoers.*

- Prov 29.4 *By justice a king gives a country stability, but one who is greedy for bribes tears it down.*
- Prov 28.5 *Evil men do not understand justice, but those who seek the Lord understand it fully.*
- Prov 29.7 *The righteous care about justice for the poor, but the wicked have no such concern.*

Leadership & Kingship

- Prov 11.14 *Without wise leadership, a nation falls; there is safety in having many advisers.*[1]
- Prov 25.2 *It is the glory of God to conceal a matter; to search out a matter is the glory of kings.*
- Prov 28.2 *When a country is rebellious, it has many rulers, but a man of understanding and knowledge maintains order.*
- Prov 29.12 *If a ruler listens to lies, all his officials become wicked.*
- Prov 31.8-9 *Speak up for those who cannot speak for themselves, for the rights of all who are destitute. Speak up and judge fairly; defend the rights of the poor and needy.*

Patience

- Prov 19.2 *It is not good to have zeal without knowledge, nor to be hasty and miss the way.*
- Prov 19.11 *A man's wisdom gives him patience; it is to his glory to overlook an offense.*
- Prov 25.15 *Through patience a ruler can be persuaded, and a gentle tongue can break a bone.*[1]

Righteous & Upright

- Prov 10.6 *Blessings crown the head of the righteous, but violence overwhelms the mouth of the wicked.*

- Prov 11.3 *The integrity of the upright guides them, but the unfaithful are destroyed by their duplicity.*

- Prov 12.28 *In the way of righteousness there is life; along that path is immortality.*

- Prov 14.32 *When calamity comes, the wicked are brought down, but even in death the righteous have a refuge.*

- Prov 15.3 *The eyes of the Lord are everywhere, keeping watch on the wicked and the good.*

- Prov 16.17 *The highway of the upright avoids evil; he who guards his way guards his life.*

- Prov 16.31 *Gray hair is the crown of splendor; it is attained by a righteous life.*

*****

When Proverbs speaks on matters of character, it is often qualified and described. At other times, there are clear warnings set forth for us when we are guilty of lacking godly character and good judgment, cursing (or afflicting) our surrounding kingdoms and communities.

Not every matter of character will be found in this chapter as some behaviors are discussed in the chapter on social issues. There, you can read about the sluggard (lazy man), the thief and robber, the mocker, the hypocrite, the unfaithful, and the wicked man.

Another chapter, titled "Warning!" is dedicated to the vast collection of verses that explicitly warn the student (us) of the consequences of adultery, drunkenness, fraudulent business practices, foolishness, pride, stubbornness, and more. These are also issues of character, but are discussed in such vivid language that I felt these warnings deserved an entire chapter of their own!

While we may look at many of these topics and believe they do not apply to us, we must honestly examine our lives and our hearts. As Christ taught in the Sermon on the Mount, anyone who looks at a woman lustfully has, in his heart, already committed adultery.[10]

It is not only in our outward actions, but the secret things of the heart where we may find ourselves described in any one of these chapters or quite possibly in all of them!

Chapter Four

CHILDREARING: AN OATMEAL SHOWER

Some people compare parenting to a marathon as opposed to a sprint. I get that, but for me, it feels more like a "Warrior Dash," an intense race through a military style obstacle course, testing the strength, agility, and endurance of the participants.

Parents, as well as athletes, start out clean and full of energy, but it doesn't take long before you get the wind knocked out of you, trip over some unseen obstacle, or get covered in muck. In fact, you probably wade through it.

It was 4 a.m. and my little toddler sat at the table beside me, cold oatmeal dripping down his head. He was crying. In fact, we both were. Everyone else in the house lay asleep, unaware of what led to such upsetting circumstances.

After all, *I* was the one who poured the oatmeal over his head.

*****

In the kitchen at zero dark thirty with my son, I was deliriously tired and felt the thick mud sucking my feet deeper and deeper into a pit. There was no pulling out, no advance, only frustration and weakening muscles. It was not my proudest moment in parenting.

In fact, I share it as an example of a, "What do I do now?" situation. He had, after all, spent half an hour begging and pleading for oatmeal. He woke up hungry in the wee hours of the morning unable to go back to sleep. To no avail, I tried to help him rest, to soothe him back to sleep. But he was insistent, demanding his beloved oatmeal. I had no other option but to make it.

However, I must explain that this is no ordinary bowl of instant oatmeal. Our family prefers a slow-cook gourmet recipe, which takes quite a bit of time and effort to produce. Imagine my surprise when after two bites, my son decided he was too tired to eat after all and refused my culinary masterpiece.

I begged, pleaded, and offered to spoon feed, but he would not have it. What he had initially demanded from me was the very thing he now refused. I snapped. I dumped it over his head, trusting that was preferable to strangling him. I had face planted in the mud.

Of course, there have been times of victory and triumph, but I don't remember those as well. And it's really annoying to hear people talk about how great of a job they've done raising their seemingly perfect kids. They make me gag! It's more interesting to hear how we all screw things up, as long as we are willing to learn from those mistakes and offer grace to others for their mistakes.

Once, after a long night at church, I was driving my children home, when my son, a little older by this time, became absolutely undone. This was a Guinness Book of World Records temper tantrum.

He didn't want to leave. When minor protests didn't work, he pulled out all the stops. As I was driving, he was thrashing, convulsing, hitting, screaming, crying, and kicking the back of my seat, staging a one man riot with alarming conviction.

My calm, reasoning voice was drowned out by his howls of discontent. He could not look at me, nor hear me. I began to worry that I couldn't drive home safely with this degree of distraction. I really wanted to spank him, right there on the side of the road, to deliver immediate consequences to his actions, but I did not want to end up on the evening news. So, I pulled over, took my cup of water, and doused him with it. Yessiree, I did!

Standing back, I watched him like a fireman observes a flame wither to smoke. Sure enough, he was so shocked out of his fit that he returned to his senses and realized that he was now soaking wet!

He began to whimper and then sob. I felt like I had broken the rules. I had done something unusual and unexpected. The idea came from left field and was just as surprising to me as it was to him.

However, I was finally able to explain why I poured water on him, and that his behavior was totally unacceptable. I reminded him that his loss of control and refusal to listen to me warranted something so unexpected. (And there was no monster-mommy story in the evening edition!)

I felt like a failure, yet the tactic worked. He became coherent. I had scaled the wall blocking my path, and now could move on. He interacted with me and stopped taking out his anger on us. We discussed his feelings of frustration and disappointment.

I was empathetic, but firm. We were going home and going to bed. Period. Then, I apologized if he was frightened by this measure.

Although my son didn't enjoy how it was accomplished, he and I had hit the reset button. He was able to both listen and (hopefully) feel that he had been heard. I still look back on that night with heartache as I felt terrible doing such a strange thing, yet it broke through his madness.

The experience allowed a reconnection and opportunity to correct misbehavior. Many would laugh at such a strange thing to do to my child. Others may be horrified and think, "how cruel, she poured *water* on him!"

Regardless of how some may judge, my son knows he is loved and cherished and that we will do anything necessary to communicate God's love and wisdom to him.

*****

I think back to many times in my life when things were not going my way and I pitched my own fit. Sadly, I had assumed God wasn't listening or responding to the tantrums of my heart. His voice did not go silent, it was just drowned out by the shouts of my own indignant protests. I too, have staged my own one woman riot.

I find it apt that Jesus calls us children of God, because much of the time, that is exactly how we behave! We see the world from our limited perspective, get bored quickly, tire easily, and create lots of messes. But our patient Father, who is *slow to anger and abounding in love*,[11] looks on us with compassion. He knows our fragility and deals with us accordingly.

There are times when we too need to be "cooled down" as Hebrews 12.10 reminds us that *God disciplines us for our good, that we may share in his holiness*. I am convinced that the love and adoration with which we shower our children cannot compare to the Father's love for each one of us!

*****

Crowning Wisdom

While Proverbs does not tell us how to handle each and every situation, it has much to say about discipline and correction. It reassures us in Prov 13.24b that *He who loves him [his son or daughter] is careful to discipline him,* and Prov 6:23b says that *the corrections of discipline are the way to life.* In short, if we love them, we must correct them through discipline.

As a former Child Protective Services Worker, I have seen firsthand how this message can easily be distorted and used as a tool to take out frustration on children. That is wrong! God tells us through James 1:19, *Everyone should be quick to listen, slow to speak and slow to become angry, for man's anger does not bring about the righteous life that God desires.* If we put this into practice in all areas of life, especially in parenting, we can avoid hurting our children when we seek to help them.

We want life and the blessings of honor, understanding, wisdom, and peace for our children. It is for their future wellbeing that we correct their errors today.

Proverbs 17.25 also warns that neglect of this *brings grief to his father and bitterness to the one who bore him.*

We have the monumental task of raising children who have hearts inclined to selfishness and sin. What complicates this task further is that we too have hearts influenced by that same sinful nature. Therefore, it is challenging. It is messy. Even exhausting and painful at times.

Sometimes we make the wrong call and have to go back and try again. Sometimes we are overprotective and waste valuable time. Sometimes we become too lax and recognize that we have missed important teaching opportunities.

We may look around and see others cruising past us and feel too weak to confront the new obstacle in our path. Yet, if we seek God's wisdom and rely on His power over sin and selfishness in our lives, we can emerge from the challenge like one completing the Warrior Dash…a little worn, a little battered, but better because of the experience. Bring out the band!

TO PARENTS & CHILDREN

- Prov 1.8-9 *My child, listen when your father corrects you. Don't neglect your mother's instruction. What you learn from them will crown you with grace and be a chain of honor around your neck.*[1]

- Prov 10.1 *A wise son brings joy to his father, but a foolish son grief to his mother.*

- Prov 13.1 *A wise son heeds his father's instruction, but a mocker doesn't listen to rebuke.*

- Prov 23.15-16 *My son, if your heart is wise, then my heart will be glad; my inmost being will rejoice when your lips speak what is right.*

- Prov 3.11-12 *My son, do not despise the Lord's discipline and do not resent His rebuke, because the Lord disciplines those He loves, as a father the son he delights in.*

DISCIPLINE & CORRECTION

- Prov 1.7 *Fear of the Lord is the foundation of true knowledge, but fools despise wisdom and discipline.*[1]

- Prov 9.8 *Do not rebuke a mocker or he will hate you; rebuke a wise man and he will love you.*
- Prov 9.9 *Instruct a wise man and he will be wiser still; teach a righteous man and he will add to his learning.*
- Prov 10.17 *He who heeds discipline shows the way to life, but whoever ignores correction leads others astray.*
- Prov 13.13 *He who scorns instruction will pay for it, but he who respects a command is rewarded.*
- Prov 13.18 *He who ignores discipline comes to poverty and shame, but whoever heeds correction is honored.*
- Prov 13.24 *Those who spare the rod of discipline hate their children. Those who love their children care enough to discipline them.*[1]
- Prov 15.5 *A fool spurns his father's discipline, but whoever heeds correction shows prudence.*
- Prov 17.10 *A rebuke impresses a man of discernment, more than a hundred lashes a fool.*
- Prov 19.18 *Discipline your children while there is hope. Otherwise you will ruin their lives.*[1]
- Prov 22.6 *Train up a child in the way he should go, and when he is old he will not turn from it.*
- Prov 22.15 *Folly is bound up in the heart of a child, but the rod of discipline will drive it far from him.*
- Prov 28.23 *He who rebukes a man will in the end gain more favor than he who has a flattering tongue.*

- Prov 29.15 *The rod of correction imparts wisdom, but a child left to himself disgraces his mother.*
- Prov 29.17 *Discipline your son, and he will give you peace; he will bring delight to your soul.*

Chapter Five

FRIENDSHIP: REINFORCEMENTS HAVE ARRIVED

A friend loves at all times, and a brother is born for adversity. Prov 17.17

Years ago, my husband was hired as a worship pastor at a church out of state. It was an exciting new ministry opportunity so we packed up our small family and moved.

It came as a terrible shock to learn that after six months, the church leadership felt that they had made a mistake in the new direction they had pursued when hiring my husband. Absent of any moral failure or impropriety, the judgment against my husband and the new direction he represented, fell quick and hard. He was forced to vacate his office and position immediately.

We felt betrayed by the very ones we trusted. There had been no warnings, no expression of misgivings by leadership, no corrective actions, no guidance or opportunity to change direction—only a termination that hit us like a ton of bricks. We found ourselves heartbroken, confused, and very alone.

Stunned, we began to call our friends and family to tell them our crushing news. Two dear friends dropped everything to rush to our side! Driving eight hours to be on our doorstep the very next morning, they expressed love and friendship to us in a way unlike ever before!

We had known them from our first years in ministry and had spent countless hours with these men and their families.

We had shared both long, difficult seasons in life and ministry as well as the joyous, inspiring seasons. We were kindred spirits, knitted together at the heart. Not only were they our friends, but brothers born for adversity.

I vividly remember the relief I felt the moment I heard the ring of our doorbell. Reinforcements had arrived!

*****

Perfume and incense bring joy to the heart, and the pleasantness of one's friend springs from his earnest counsel. Prov 27.9

As we greeted them, our tears flowed and we felt the warm embrace of love and cheer. They sat and listened to our news, lamented with us over our heartache, and prayed with us for wisdom, peace, and provision.

There were no assumptions of guilt or wrongdoing, just love and support. They offered wisdom and godly counsel on how to proceed from that point with integrity in spite of our thirst for retaliation. Our anxiety began to melt away and peace was restored in spite of the difficult situation we still faced.

Solomon wrote about our need for friends in Ecclesiastes 4.9-10,12:

Two are better than one, because they have a good return for their work: If one falls down, his friend can help him up. But pity the man who falls and has no one to help him up...Though one may be overpowered, two can defend themselves. A cord of three strands is not quickly broken.

Our friends had come to help us up. Unfortunately, a man named Job had a much different response from his friends after a disastrous string of life altering events.

*****

[What] miserable comforters you are! Will your long-winded speeches never end? Job 16:2b-3a

Job was righteous, God fearing, and very, very wealthy. One day, Satan approached God and insisted that Job's loyalty was only based on God's material blessings.

So God gave Satan permission to test Job. In one day, all of Job's livestock (and livelihood) was either stolen or destroyed. Then, a sudden storm leveled the home of his oldest son, killing all of Job's children.

After that, Satan inflicted Job with painful sores over his entire body. These intensified over time, producing broken skin and festering sores, covered by worms and scabs.

Job could not sleep. He was tormented by dreams and visions and was so distressed he could not eat. Job became gaunt and emaciated from malnutrition and weakened from the lack of sleep. He had been deserted by his kinsmen, servants, and brothers. Even his wife was repulsed by his condition.

His life, livelihood, and reputation were ruined. Job was broken.

Then Job's friends enter the scene in Job 2.11-13:

When Job's three friends, Eliphaz, Bildad, and Zophar, heard about all the troubles that had come upon him, they set out from their homes and met together by agreement to

go and sympathize with him and comfort him. When they saw him from a distance, they could hardly recognize him; they began to weep aloud, and they tore their robes and sprinkled dust on their heads. Then they sat on the ground with him for seven days and seven nights. No one said a word to him, because they saw how great his suffering was.

They sound like great friends so far, right? However, as the story continues, their attitudes shifted from compassion to condemnation.

Eliphaz, the first friend to speak, initially encouraged Job but then suggested that he might possibly be *reaping what he has sown*. Bildad spoke up next and sharply rebuked Job and his deceased children, assuming some type of flagrant violation: *When your children sinned against him [God], he gave them over to the penalty of their sin.*[12] Ouch.

Then Zophar jumped on the bandwagon and upped the ante. He ruthlessly accused Job of mocking God! They continued heaping condemnation on Job insisting that he repent of his wrongdoing. Presumably, Job must have been guilty of some gross defiance against God, as this appalling fate could only be due to one who was evil and had never even known God.[13]

Wow, with friends like these, who needs enemies?

*****

Acquitting the guilty and condemning the innocent—the Lord detests them both.
Prov 17.15

It is a difficult task navigating the ups and downs, twists and turns of the various seasons of life. Our days are filled with blessings, tests, trainings, and trials. My husband and I feel richly blessed by the friends God has placed in our lives during the good, the bad, and the baffling.

In fact, we might not have remained in ministry at all if we did not have friends who came alongside us during difficult times. Their faith in us and in a Sovereign God brought great peace and joy to us.

Eventually Job heard from God Himself in a storm.

It was awesome, yet downright terrifying! Although Job never cursed God and had done nothing deserving of such suffering, he did assume that God had turned on him. His friends were *miserable comforters,* condemning an innocent man, and totally off base about what God was doing in his life.

How many times do we do the same to our hurting friends?

In the end, God spoke to those friends in the storm too, and He confronted them with their mischaracterization and misinterpretation of Him. As a result, God would only accept Job's sacrifices and prayers on their behalf before He forgave their foolishness! Wow!

And, of course, Job was restored. He went on to father ten more children, and received back even greater blessings of wealth, honor, and longevity after he repented of his attitude, acknowledging the goodness and greatness of God. He was made prosperous again, enjoying twice as much as he had lost, and lived to see the fourth generation of his new children.

*****

An anxious heart weighs a man down, but a kind word cheers him up. Prov 12.25

Our stories don't always have a happy ending here on earth. People will hurt us. We may hurt them too. It may not be intentional or even obvious. But we desperately need friends. Everyone needs relationships and brotherhood.

Paul told the church at Colosse to be clothed with *compassion, kindness, humility, gentleness, and patience. Bear with each other and forgive whatever grievances you may have against one another. Forgive as the Lord forgave you. And over all these virtues, put on love, which binds them all together in perfect unity.*[14]

Bear with each other. Forgive. Put on love. Be united.

To love others is the greatest command second only to loving God.

Although we have never received any apologies from those who hurt us in our early years of ministry, we have forgiven them. It has taken time, prayer, and discipline. Occasionally, the enemy tries to reignite old emotions and pain from that experience, revealing to us that forgiveness is not a one-time thing. Sometimes it must be done daily. Or hourly.

Today, we look back on those experiences with an entirely different perspective. Our faith was strengthened unlike any other experience we share. We learned valuable lessons in leadership, ministry, and friendship that inspire my husband to be the best shepherd he can be to his own staff today.

*****

Crowning Wisdom

Proverbs guides us in our friendships by helping us identify if our actions or the actions of others are that of love and true friendship. Quite often, the Proverbs sound like an example of what not to do in friendship, while other passages directly promote attributes such as: kindness that leads to respect, reliance on one's friend nearby as opposed to the brother far away, and the value of a friend who keeps us sharp, even wounding us when necessary. Those relationships are most beneficial as those "wounds" strengthen and prove love in friendship as opposed to the falsehood of enemies who never warn us of danger ahead, yet continue to *multiply kisses*.

The verses below address the treatment of our neighbors, or other people in general. This could be anyone: friend, foe, and those who might actually be a little of both, like Job's.

FRIENDS, NEIGHBORS & RANDOM CITIZENS

- Prov 3.27-28 *Do not withhold good from those who deserve it, when it is in your power to act. Do not say to your neighbor, "Come back later, I'll give it to you tomorrow," when you now have it with you.*

- Prov 6.16-19 *There are six things the Lord hates—no, seven things he detests: haughty eyes, a lying tongue, hands that kill the innocent, a heart that plots evil, feet that race to do wrong, a false witness who pours out lies, a person who sows discord in a family.*[1]

- Prov 18.24 *A man of many companions may come to ruin, but there is a friend who sticks closer than a brother.*
- Prov 19.11 *A man's wisdom gives him patience, it is to his glory to overlook an offense.*
- Prov 19.17 *He who is kind to the poor lends to the Lord, and he will reward him for what he has done.*
- Prov 22.24-26 *Do not make friends with a hot-tempered man, do not associate with one easily angered, or you may learn his ways and get yourself ensnared.*
- Prov 25.9-10 *If you argue your case with a neighbor, do not betray another man's confidence, or he who hears it may shame you and you will never lose your bad reputation.*
- Prov 27.5-6 *Better is open rebuke than hidden love. Wounds from a friend can be trusted, but an enemy multiplies kisses.*
- Prov 27.7 *He who is full loathes honey, but to the hungry even what is bitter tastes sweet.*
- Prov 27.10 *Do not forsake your friend and the friend of your father and do not go to your brother's house when disaster strikes you—better a neighbor nearby than a brother far away.*
- Prov 27.17 *As iron sharpens iron, so one man sharpens another.*

Chapter Six

LIFE: OUTSIDE OF EDEN

Life is sometimes hard to figure out. I was 19 years old when I married my husband, who was one week shy of his 19th birthday.

We were so young that, essentially, we grew up together. And our marriage has certainly been through infancy, childhood, and some tumultuous adolescence. As literal teenagers and young adults, we believed that as long as we loved each other and stuck together, we would be fine. However, our Beatles' "Love Is All You Need" theory was proven wrong by the hardships we have faced, our search for purpose, and the challenges of living this side of Eden.

A few obstacles we faced stemmed from our obvious financial unpreparedness and irresponsibility. Establishing a household took more than we had expected yet less than we actually required. We have since learned from our mistakes and work hard not to repeat the foolish choices that cost us dearly.

However, a less than obvious challenge in our young marriage was loneliness. At nineteen, all of our friends were either at college, working, or partying. We had postponed children until our educations were complete so we had lots of time on our hands. We had no other married couples our age to spend evenings and weekends with for fun and amusement. And when we did go out with unmarried friends, it was awkward and forced. We felt like we were on display like road signs, either directing drivers on a scenic route to marital bliss or warning of dangerous roads ahead.

We also struggled for years to discern what God wanted us to do with our lives. It is one thing to seek God's will for your life as an individual but another thing entirely when you are married and seeking direction as a couple.

Eventually we felt led towards ministry, which posed an increased challenge for us as newlyweds. Transitional ministries, multiple relocations, and financial ruin brought immense pressure that we were unable to bear on our own. There was also grief from circumstances beyond our control, such as pregnancy loss, an unexpected job termination, health problems, and a failed church plant.

Clearly, love was not all we needed!

*****

Many are the plans in a man's heart, but it is the Lord's purpose that prevails. Prov 19.21

As we looked around, we began to feel discouraged, stuck in limbo, as we perceived that everyone else had life figured out. No one was asking the same questions that plagued our hearts. Who are we to be now that we are a "we" and not a "me?" What does God want us to do with our lives?

We were naïve and assumed that we alone struggled with identity, responsibility, and purpose. Weren't we "adults" now—married, working, and planning for the future?

But our plans never seemed to work out. Our ideas and dreams seemed to be lacking something. Significance. Value. Purpose. Maybe even God.

We began to ponder, "What is life really about? Did God intend for life to be a constant struggle? Were these difficulties particular to us or universal and common to everyone? Or worse, had we become so privileged, used to things coming easily in our Western culture, that we would never be deeply satisfied?"

*****

The wise woman builds her house, but with her own hands, the foolish one tears hers down.
Prov 14.1

It wasn't until we revisited the story of Creation (see Appendix) and original sin that something occurred to us. Mankind's true purpose, the life God originally designed for us, was actually much simpler and doubtlessly more beautiful than what anyone experiences today.

We considered the life given to Adam and Eve. Theirs was extravagant, lovely, and tranquil. Their job was simple: to care for God's beautiful garden. They existed to enjoy God and His beautiful new world. Period.

Their identity was secure in their relationship with the Creator. He gave them purpose, value, and significance by giving them responsibility and dominion over all creation. Their work was a joy and their resources limitless.

Eden itself was designed to sheer perfection and comfort, so much so that Adam and Eve didn't even need clothing! They innocently wandered through God's paradise with the same delight as a nude toddler playing in the sprinkler on a hot summer day. He created them to live naked and free in the Garden.

But the home that God gave them in Eden was destroyed by one fatal decision. Eve was deceived by Satan and chose to know both good and evil rather than remain innocent and pure. She was foolish and tore down everything God had built for her and Adam. As a result, their nakedness, a blessing in their innocence, became a burden, marked by their guilt and shame.

*****

We were made for Eden. But that's not where we live today. Presently, mankind faces hard work and toil, natural and man-made disasters, violence, jealousy, quarreling, murder, immorality, sexual degradation, abuse, sickness, and death. And women are all painfully aware of their particular curse in increased pains in childbearing.

Now about that curse. Personally, I thought "come on, it can't be THAT bad," so I planned to give birth naturally and experience the full beauty of the miracle of childbirth. Cue the violins.

I was doing fine until I thought our daughter was going to come out of my back instead of where God intended.

I tried it all: rocking, walking, squatting, focused breathing. But it didn't stop the feeling of a locomotive ripping through my body. So I caved. I couldn't take it anymore. I accepted the drugs. Truthfully, I would have taken anything at that moment if they told me it would stop the pain. Yet when the magical shot IN MY SPINE didn't work, I panicked and asked for a gun. (Although I didn't grow up on a farm, it was pretty rural nonetheless, so I was no stranger to puttin' animals out of their misery.) I begged my husband, "Kill me, kill me now! Save the baby!"

Yes, we women will all thank Eve when we get to heaven, but for now, we have to figure this place out. We must build a home here for now. Outside of Eden.

*****

We could easily despair in our dying bodies and in this broken down world—and many do. However, the apostle Paul writes words of hope and reassurance in 2 Corinthians 5.1,4:

Now we know that if the earthly tent we live in is destroyed, we have a building from God, an eternal house in heaven, not built by human hands...For while we are in this tent, we groan and are burdened, because we do not wish to be unclothed but to be clothed with our heavenly dwelling, so that what is mortal may be swallowed up by life.

And we do groan. We groan when children die of starvation, when innocent blood is shed, and when justice is not served. We groan when our bodies, our earthly tents, succumb to illness and disease. We groan when we fail and feel the weight of our sinfulness. We groan because spiritually speaking, without Christ's covering, we, like Adam and Eve, are naked, exposed, and vulnerable to sin and its injury.

The earth also groans *as in the pains of childbirth* and is desperate for our eternal reconciliation with God. One day, *Creation itself will be liberated from its bondage to decay and brought into the glorious freedom of the children of God.*[15] Yes, earth too will be transformed and renewed, never again to be subject to the frustration of the curse of sin!

And so we wait. All creation and Christ followers wait expectantly; that's why the writer compared it to the pains of childbirth. We are "expecting." We confidently wait for the promised redemption of our bodies and possess His Spirit within us as collateral: *Now it is God who has made us for this very purpose and has given us the Spirit as a deposit, guaranteeing what is to come.* 2 Corinthians 5.5

Meanwhile, we desire to be clothed in His righteousness and life. Paul, in Romans 13.14, urges us to *clothe yourselves with the Lord Jesus Christ*[1] and in Colossians 3.12, *clothe yourselves with compassion, kindness, humility, gentleness, and patience.*

We no longer want this nakedness and an earthly tent that is so easily destroyed. We long for our heavenly dwelling. We cry out and wait expectantly for the life He intended for us initially, but will once again deliver...for eternity.

*****

Her [Wisdom's] ways are pleasant ways, and all her paths are peace. She is a tree of life to those who embrace her; those who lay hold of her will be blessed. Prov 3.17-18

His Word gives wisdom, a metaphorical new tree of life, for not only living, but also thriving, in a dying world! Regardless of how difficult the path may become at times, we have the peace and security from the one who guides and preserves us through it. Although He does not eliminate all adversity from our lives, He promises to go before us and fill us with His peace each step of the way.

Taking hold of wisdom as tightly as we can leads to a life filled with blessings that far outweigh our temporary setbacks.

*****

Crowning Wisdom

Some may say that love is all you need to remain strong and hopeful in this life. I guess it depends on whose love you're talking about. Our love is limited and often based on circumstances and emotion.

God's love is unlimited, unconditional, and unchanging. That is what sustains us through our trials, disappointment, and failures this side of Eden.

The following selection of verses addresses life from both philosophical and practical points of view. It covers the attitude and state of our hearts, our home life, and our ability to love.

I am confident the Proverbs can help us cultivate lives that still flourish, like a tree of life, giving fruit in every season, filling the world with His beauty, creativity, and extravagant love. We just need to embrace wisdom and expect His blessings to follow!

Let the wise listen to these Proverbs and become wiser... Prov 1.5

LIFE

- Prov 14.30 *A heart at peace gives life to the body, but envy rots the bones.*

- Prov 15.24 *The path of life leads upward for the wise to keep him from going down to the grave.*

- Prov 16.3 *Commit to the Lord whatever you do, and your plans will succeed.*

- Prov 16.20 *Whoever gives heed to instruction prospers, and blessed is he who trusts in the Lord.*

- Prov 20.13 *Do not love sleep or you will grow poor; stay awake and you will have food to spare.*

- Prov 21.2 *People may be right in their own eyes, but the Lord examines their heart.*[1]

- Prov 22.1 *A good name is more desirable than great riches; to be esteemed is better than silver or gold.*

- Prov 22.4 *Humility and the fear of the Lord bring wealth and honor and life.*

Balance & Moderation

- Prov 25.16-17 *If you find honey, eat just enough—too much of it, and you will vomit. Seldom set foot in your neighbor's house—too much of you, and he will hate you.*

Dissatisfaction

- Prov 27.20 *Just as Death and Destruction are never satisfied, so human desire is never satisfied.*[1]

Heart & Spirit

- Prov 14.10 *Each heart knows its own bitterness, and no one else can share its joy.*

- Prov 15.13 *A happy heart makes the face cheerful, but heartache crushes the spirit.*

- Prov 17.3 *The crucible for silver, the furnace for gold, but the Lord tests the heart.*

- Prov 17.22 *A cheerful heart is good medicine, but a crushed spirit dries up the bones.*

- Prov 27.19 *As water reflects a face, so a man's heart reflects the man.*

The Home & Homestead

- Prov 15.6 *The house of the righteous contains great treasure, but the income of the wicked brings them trouble.*

- Prov 17.1 *Better a dry crust with peace and quiet than a house with feasting and strife.*

Love

- Prov 3.3-4 *Let love and faithfulness never leave you; bind them around your neck, write them on the tablet of your heart. Then you will win favor and a good name in the sight of God and man.*

- Prov 10.12 *Hatred stirs up dissension, but love covers over all wrongs.*

- Prov 17.9 *He who covers an offense promotes love, but whoever repeats the matter separates close friends.*

Priorities

- Prov 24.27 *Finish your outdoor work and get your fields ready; after that, build your house.*

- Prov 21.17 *He who loves pleasure will become poor, whoever loves wine and oil will never be rich.*

Purpose & Duty

- Prov 20.5 *The purposes of a man's heart are deep waters, but a man of understanding draws them out.*

Work

- Prov 12.24 *Diligent hands will rule, but laziness ends in slave labor.*
- Prov 14.23 *All hard work brings a profit, but mere talk leads only to poverty.*
- Prov 18.9 *One who is slack in his work is brother to one who destroys.*
- Prov 10.5 *He who gathers crops in summer is a wise son, but he who sleeps during harvest is a disgraceful son.*
- Prov 28.19 *He who works his land will have abundant food, but the one who chases fantasies will have his fill of poverty.*

Chapter Seven

SOCIAL ISSUES: BREAKING THE CYCLE

As a social worker in my early twenties, I worked with families who had neglected or abused their children. It was incredibly difficult. Social work shined a spotlight on the depravity of mankind and the darkness of all our hearts.

While training for this job, I was often challenged to recognize the strengths within a family and work from there.

My problem, however, was that I have always been a realist, not an optimist. When interacting with client families, I saw the reality of the unfortunate, the foolish, and the entitled. Instead of celebrating how far they had come, I struggled with the remaining distance they must go.

I entered social work hoping to make the world a better place for others; however, I found that the tools I was given were entirely ineffective. The complexity of the cases was overwhelming; most parents faced enormous barriers and challenges brought on by poor choices, weak support systems, and limited options. Others had experienced great loss, tragedy, and just seemed to be cursed. Some were relegated to poverty and dependence by exploitation or poor leadership of those they depended upon.

Personally, I struggled with understanding why my life and circumstances seemed so favorable and blessed, while others' were so diametrically opposite. I am undeserving of the blessings I have received, yet to me, they were just as undeserving of such misfortune.

While some clients worked very hard and were grateful for our support, others were resentful, antagonistic, and refused to acknowledge their dire circumstances or toxic relationships. The average social worker quits or transfers after just three years.

*****

The most disturbing cases to me were those of sexual abuse. According to the Centers for Disease Control, one out of four girls is sexually abused before she reaches the age of eighteen. One in every four! If you have four daughters, that's one of your own statistically speaking! Many believe this statistic is actually higher as there are countless cases that go unreported every year!

But hold on, it gets worse. According to Mary Frances Bowley, author of *The White Umbrella*, "The damage from just one incident is life altering. Emotionally, girls are arrested [halted] in their development and make choices [later] based on their emotional age at the time of abuse."[16] I was confounded when I learned that many children would tell a parent about the sexual abuse, but the parent (often the mother) would not believe the child or take any action against the perpetrator. WHY?

It typically came down to two reasons. Primarily, she was in some way dependent on the abuser: financially, emotionally, or sexually. She would have to choose her child over her mate and face a difficult road alone. Many feel they do not have the financial resources, courage, and ability to navigate life without a mate. So the child suffers.

Secondarily, some mothers had themselves been victimized at a young age. If they were not protected and given treatment, they succumbed to bitterness and resignation. In essence, they had become arrested emotionally and developmentally, incapable of taking assertive action to protect their own victimized child. And so the cycle continues.

But it doesn't have to be that way.

*****

I have a friend. She is older and much wiser than me. She and her husband are one of the few older couples in our predominantly young family church. I lovingly refer to them as "kids" because they remind me of teenagers deeply in love, and they are full of energy, enthusiasm, and sharp wit. They pull no punches and I love that about them!

I will call my friend "Grace."

Grace is a survivor of sexual abuse. It began around the age of five. Like many of my former clients, she told her mother about the abuse she and her twin had endured, but instead of responding, Grace's mother ignored this painful disclosure and avoided action.

They told no one else. The thought of bringing ruin to their family prevented any notions of disclosure to classmates, their church community, or even to their loving grandmother who lived nearby.

Throughout their childhood, Grace and her twin lived in constant fear of their mercurial father. Each family member served him and worked tirelessly to avoid upsetting him. They could not predict whom they would encounter from day to day—Dr. Jekyll or Mr. Hyde.

On their massive farm, the twins often sought refuge in the many barns, silos, and wooded areas to avoid the likelihood of another incident of sexual abuse. But it rarely worked. Father always seemed to find one of them. And no matter how they sidestepped, no matter how they resisted, no matter how they despised these encounters, fear and intimidation left them defenseless.

After eleven years of avoidance, despair, and exhaustion, they realized that no one would end this or advocate for their safety. So Grace finally took an enormous risk.

One day, before another likely incident, Grace opposed their coercive father, threatened abandonment, and faced down the very one who had violently robbed them of all confidence, security, and self-worth.

By the grace of God that was all it took!

Talk about moxie! The abuse ceased! But their offender remained. The betrayal remained. The pain remained.

*****

Grace eventually graduated high school, attended college, married, and had children. She describes parenting as "traumatic" for her, reflecting on the shell of a person she had become. "I wasn't 'present'...I wasn't my authentic self."

Plagued with doubt and insecurity, she constantly wondered how to be a good mother as there was little to draw upon instinctually. Her mother modeled the busy caregiver that provided materially for her children but clearly was not available emotionally or spiritually.

Yet Grace determined to be different. She would read to her children, although no one had read to her. She would sit on the edge of their bed and comfort them when they were frightened, sad, or overwhelmed. She would make them feel valued and special, safe and secure. She would do many of the things her mother failed to do, but someone else had done for her. Her grandmother.

Grammie lived on the adjacent farm. She gave Grace and her sister a safe haven, a soft place to fall. At Grammie's they were embraced and comforted. She also spoke of God in a different way than others in her life, "Grammie would walk out and say, 'Look what a beautiful day God gave me! Look what beautiful flowers God gave me!'"

*****

After fifteen years of marriage, Grace's twin experienced a personal crisis and determined to finally confront their mother with her culpability during the years of abuse. Grace traveled to support her twin and the efforts she was making to confront her past, but little did Grace know that this was the beginning of her own journey to recovery.

Ben, Grace's husband, had not known about the sexual abuse. He knew of their father's intimidation and violent temper and how he disparaged their mother and everyone else in the home, but Ben was unaware of the sexual abuse.

He did not shy away from Grace as many men do, but he walked with her, every painful step of emotional, psychological, and spiritual recovery. As with most cases of sustained long term abuse, the recovery was neither quick nor easy.

It cost a lot too. Through many stops and starts, roadblocks and transfers, the decade long quest for recovery was expensive, time intensive, and challenging, to say the least. But Ben considered his bride valuable enough to do whatever it would take to see her restored.

*****

One of the most interesting steps in Grace's therapy was to buy a doll that represented her inner child. It was to look like Grace as a child and somehow embody the young girl who had been lost to betrayal and abuse.

She found one with long braided pigtails and blue and white striped overalls. Having lived on a farm, this was a striking representation of her young self.

The assignment was to start self-conversations—to talk to her inner child. "If you belonged to me this would never have happened...and this will never happen to you again...I will not let this happen to you again." Ultimately, she would speak words of trust, security, and reassurance to the frightened little girl that had been halted by trauma, frozen in time, and arrested from developing into the confident and secure woman she longed to be.

This assignment was a game changer for Grace. No longer did she feel like the helpless victim, but she finally saw in herself the amazing courage and strength that had been there all along. She recognized, in that little girl, the incredible strength she exerted to survive and ultimately stop the abuse once and for all.

*****

There were, of course, other tasks. Other assignments. More work to address the betrayal, the anger, the years of violation she and her twin endured. And she would have to eventually forgive if she was to fully experience freedom and restoration.

But the father was not the one she struggled to forgive. The love she had for him died long ago in the abuse, and any emotional connections to him were severed such that she viewed him detachedly, as an outsider and someone who didn't know any better. To Grace, it was easier to forgive him than someone else whose betrayal still haunts her to this day, that of her mother.

Long into therapy, she confronted her mother about her inaction. "Why didn't you do anything?" she asked.

Defensively, her mother responded, "What did you expect me to do? Where would I go? What was I supposed to do?"

The greatest barrier to Grace's recovery was forgiveness. She just couldn't do it. She couldn't forgive the one person she had entrusted with this painful disclosure, but had refused to intervene. Her mother did not deserve forgiveness and wasn't even asking for forgiveness. The resentment Grace carried was holding her hostage—keeping her from recovery.

For over a year, she tried to forgive. Her counselor offered every possible path toward forgiveness, to no avail. It was tripping her up, holding her prisoner though she struggled for freedom. Exasperated, she advised Grace, "You are going to have to pray, to ask God to help you forgive her."

So she did. Miraculously, her prayer was answered, and almost overnight, Grace was released from the bitterness and resentment she held for her mother.

Finally, it was gone. The animosity towards her mother was replaced by peace, compassion, and forgiveness. What she struggled to do in her own strength for over a year, God accomplished in His strength overnight.

In no way does Grace condone her mother's failure to protect them, but she sees through aging eyes filled with knowledge, experience, and insight. She views the poor decisions of her mother as evidence of a woman who had also been beaten down, lacking the self-worth and confidence to defend herself, let alone her vulnerable children.

Slowly, the weight of her past began to lift from her shoulders. Grace no longer bore the burden of inappropriate guilt. She no longer felt shame for the sins of another perpetrated against her. She no longer hated her mother for failing to end the abuse. Grace was no longer arrested by the trauma, imprisoned by fear. She was free!

*****

In retrospect, Grace sees the hand of God at work throughout all of these experiences, the good and the bad. She does not waste time asking God why He let the abuse happen. She thanks Him that it ended.

She doesn't complain that her treatment took nearly a decade; she appreciates His guidance and presence in the process.

She doesn't live as one stuck, broken, or victimized. She lives as a child of God who has experienced healing, resumed growth, and been renewed!

Today, she glows! You would never suspect this woman is a survivor of abuse. Her optimism and sense of humor are infectious, and her no-holds-barred approach to everything reminds me of the boldness of an innocent child. You know the kind of child that boasts of her big powerful dad that can overcome anything and anyone? But the dad she boasts of is not her earthly father—it's her Heavenly Father.

She embodies the Scriptures where Jesus told his disciples, *unless you change and become like little children, you will never enter the kingdom of heaven.*[17] But Jesus wasn't suggesting that we revert back to our childhoods, shirk responsibility, or just try to ignore or forget our pain. He urges us to trust him with the absolute faith a child places in her parent.

Our Heavenly Father looks down on His children, embraces us like Grace embraced that little doll, and says things like, "You belong to me. I never wanted these terrible things to happen to you, but you have been brave. Let me make it right. I have seen everything and will hold them to account. I will fix your crushed heart and make it stronger and more beautiful than before. I am able. Trust me. You are my child, and I love you more than you can imagine."

*****

Speak up for those who cannot speak for themselves; ensure justice for those being crushed. Yes, speak up for the poor and helpless, and see that they get justice. Prov 31.8-9[1]

The cycle can be broken. God can take our fractured lives and restore us to health and vitality. Social work alone cannot do it. He can take the addict, dependent, and abuser and fill the voids driving their destructive behaviors. Programs alone cannot do it. He can take an aimless life and give it purpose. He takes the orphans, homeless, and unloved and makes them His treasured children. Shelters, homes, and services alone cannot do it.

I do not argue against social work as I do see it as a vital service to vulnerable populations. We must continue to work to protect at-risk children and even aging adults from abusers. Scripture charges us to speak up for those who cannot speak for themselves—to defend the defenseless, to seek justice for the oppressed, and to help the needy.

However, I find that much of our public assistance only addresses symptoms of a greater problem, a deeper wound.

That wound is our sin nature. If left unchallenged, it can lead us to be abusive, cause us to neglect our work and responsibilities, direct us to negative coping mechanisms such as avoidance, anger, denial, or substance abuse.

Our sinful nature leads us to self-destruct. That is its ultimate purpose: to destroy God's creation and image bearers.

Today, I am no longer a Child Protective Services Worker. I am a homemaker, writer, seasonal homeschooling mother, and I lead a women's group at church. However, I have not forgotten great lessons from my days in social work.

I realize that I did nothing to deserve loving, protective parents that led me in faith and wisdom, but I will do anything to share my faith and wisdom with others. I realize that I struggle against the same selfish, sinful nature as my former perpetrator clients. I realize that beneath it all, we are all people and we all have issues.

*****

Crowning Wisdom

To heal the brokenness of our hearts, we must seek wisdom from the Creator of our hearts. We must seek restoration and rely on the One from whom wisdom originated.

Proverbs is an excellent source of godly wisdom that exposes many of the social issues and deleterious choices we make today. Don't we often seek security and dependency in others as opposed to Christ? Wouldn't we rather ignore our spiritual condition and blame our church leaders, rather than take responsibility for it ourselves? Aren't we all, at times, lazy when we should instead be diligent? How often do we take from others, scoff at correction, or meddle in other's affairs when Scripture tells us clearly that these are destructive attitudes and tendencies? How much do we resemble the wicked when we are called to be holy?

Proverbs helps us recognize the direction of our hearts and assess whether we are merely victims of our sin nature, arrested in our development, or perpetrators of destruction. I believe it to be our best source of protection, growth, healing, and hope.

BUSYBODY & MEDDLER

- Prov 26.17 *Like one who seizes a dog by the ears is a passer-by who meddles in a quarrel not his own.*

THE HYPOCRITE

- Prov 28.13 *He who conceals his sins does not prosper, but whoever confesses and renounces them finds mercy.*

THE MISCHIEVOUS & TROUBLEMAKER

- Prov 26.18-19 *Like a madman shooting firebrands or deadly arrows is a man who deceives his neighbor and says, "I was only joking!"*

MOCKERS & SCOFFERS

- Prov 9.7 *Whoever corrects a mocker invites insult; whoever rebukes a wicked man incurs abuse.*

- Prov 14.6 *The mocker seeks wisdom and finds none, but knowledge comes easily to the discerning.*
- Prov 20.1 *Wine is a mocker and beer a brawler; whoever is led astray by them is not wise.*
- Prov 29.8 *Mockers stir up a city, but wise men turn away anger.*

Thief & Robber

- Prov 28.24 *He who robs his father or mother and says, "It's not wrong"—he is partner to him who destroys.*
- Prov 29.24 *The accomplice of a thief is his own enemy; he is put under oath and dares not testify.*

Laziness & the Sluggard

- Prov 6.6-8 *Go to the ant, you sluggard; consider its ways and be wise! It has no commander, no overseer, or ruler, yet it stores its provisions in summer and gathers its food at harvest.*
- Prov 20.4 *A sluggard does not plow in season; so at harvest time he looks but finds nothing.*
- Prov 20.13 *Do not love sleep or you will grow poor; stay awake and you will have food to spare.*
- Prov 24.30-34 *I went past the field of the sluggard, past the vineyard of the man who lacks judgment; thorns had come up everywhere, the ground was covered with weeds, and the stone wall was in ruins. I applied my heart to what I observed and learned a lesson from what I saw: a little sleep, a little slumber, a little*

folding of the hands to rest—and poverty will come on you like a bandit and scarcity like an armed man.

- Prov 26.14 *As a door turns on its hinges, so a sluggard turns on his bed.*

THE UNFAITHFUL

- Prov 11.6 *The righteousness of the upright delivers them, but the unfaithful are trapped by evil desires.*
- Prov 25.19 *Like a bad tooth or a lame foot is reliance on the unfaithful in times of trouble.*

WICKEDNESS & EVIL

- Prov 5.22 *The evil deeds of a wicked man ensnare him; the cords of his sin hold him fast.*
- Prov 11.21 *Be sure of this: The wicked will not go unpunished, but those who are righteous will go free.*
- Prov 12.20 *There is deceit in the heart of those who plot evil, but joy for those who promote peace.*
- Prov 15.3 *The eyes of the Lord are everywhere, keeping watch on the wicked and the good.*
- Prov 21.12 *The Righteous One takes note of the house of the wicked and brings the wicked to ruin.*
- Prov 24.1-2 *Do not envy wicked men, do not desire their company; for their hearts plot violence, and their lips talk about making trouble.*
- Prov 28.1 *The wicked man flees though no one pursues, but the righteous are as bold as a lion.*

- Prov 28.10 *He who leads the upright along an evil path will fall into his own trap, but the blameless will receive a good inheritance.*

- Prov 29.6 *An evil man is snared by his own sin, but a righteous one can sing and be glad.*

Chapter Eight

TONGUE & SPEECH: A RESTLESS EVIL

Reckless words pierce like a sword, but the tongue of the wise brings healing. Prov 12.18

Can you think back to that time in school when someone said or did something that utterly humiliated you? There are many for me, but one stands out from the rest.

I was awkwardly attempting to flirt with a guy in high school, and it was misunderstood and rejected. Before I knew it, I was the object of public ridicule. I escaped to the restroom to hide my tears and catch my breath as I began dry heaving. I still remember the horror I felt at such public disgrace. The words he spoke were not only a mockery of me, but they were announced for all to hear. I have never forgotten it.

Of course, this was before the internet, social media, the invisible "cloud" that I still don't quite understand, and a worldwide platform for anyone to post their most scathing criticism and ridicule of others. I can only imagine how intensified my feelings would have been had there been an online forum for sharing the most heinous missteps of my youth or a broader audience for my premature beliefs and opinions of others.

Recently, a popular social media account was set up targeting students at a school in our district. The user name and password were given out in a post, in essence, creating a billboard for posting any students' most embarrassing moments, identifying them by name, and even reporting on their private sexual activity. Its very creation was for the express purpose of humiliating and degrading others.

What is happening today? Are we unaware of the power of our words, becoming lazy and reckless, or simply callous and uncaring?

*****

The tongue has the power of life and death, and those who love it will eat its fruit. Prov 18.21

Words are powerful. As Prov 15.4 asserts, *The tongue that brings healing is a tree of life, but a deceitful tongue crushes the spirit.* The Hebrew word for crushing is *shêber*, which means to fracture, afflict, destroy, ruin. These are not superficial injuries but painful blows that penetrate the heart and soul, sustaining crippling damage equivalent to a fractured or crushed bone.

The way we communicate, our intent, and how it is received impact the hearer and the speaker. Our words have the capacity to soothe and restore or to smash and destroy.

They have the power to give life or death.

*****

He who guards his lips guards his life, but he who speaks rashly will come to ruin. Prov 13.3

James, the half-brother of Jesus, author of the New Testament book of James, leader of the church in Jerusalem, and Christian martyr, is lovingly dubbed "Pastor Jimmy" in our home. His writing reminds me of a deacon or pastor similar to those from my Southern Baptist upbringing. I envision him as a loving yet stern older gentleman, agitated, perhaps, by the lack of understanding from his congregants.

He writes as if he has had to straighten out more than a few misconceptions. James spoke with great authority, passion, and concern that give me pause when I consider my own words in conversation and criticism. James 3.5-8 cautions us:

> *The tongue is a small part of the body, but it makes great boasts. Consider what a great forest is set on fire by a small spark. The tongue also is a fire, a world of evil among the parts of the body. It corrupts the whole person, sets the whole course of his life on fire, and is itself set on fire by hell. All kinds of animals, birds, reptiles, and sea creatures are being tamed and have been tamed by mankind, but no human being can tame the tongue. It is a restless evil, full of deadly poison.*

Wow. A world of evil among the parts of the body. A restless evil, full of deadly poison. A hungry fire. An untamable beast. This is hyperbole, right? Surely he doesn't mean that we carry around with us a match, lit and ready to ignite anything it touches? I guess that depends on whether or not you agree with the old nursery rhyme, "sticks and stones may break my bones, but words will never hurt me."

Actually, I think if James had lived today, he would have called the tongue a live grenade, pin pulled, and ready for the drop. And worse, he warned that the damage is not only to the victim of our careless, destructive words, but to the speaker as well, *It corrupts the whole person, sets the whole course of his life on fire.* Pastor Jimmy doesn't mince words or offer ignorance as an excuse. He is sounding the alarm and urging us to safety.

But for those who believe that this sounds like an overabundance of caution and need further evidence, Prov 18.7 also predicts, *A fool's mouth is his undoing, and his lips are a snare to his soul.*

I doubt we consider the harm that is to come to ourselves when we utter that tiny bit of gossip, tell that little white lie, or criticize another. Yet, scripture unequivocally tells us that we entrap and bring harm to ourselves as well as others when we do not keep our tongue in check.

Unfortunately, many of us grossly underestimate the impact of our words to strangers, work associates, friends (both online and offline), spouses, and our children. I admit that it's hard to fully appreciate. How could sound waves, letters on a screen, or words on paper have any lasting impact on anyone at all?

One of the most popular AT&T advertising campaigns featured the tagline, "that was so thirty seconds ago." The concept was brilliant and its pervasive truth satirized our drive to keep up with the rapid rate of changing technology. It mocked anything that didn't function at the speed of the latest 4G network, including personal conversations.

It appears to me that many of us now view our words much the same way, "Sure, I said I was leaving you and the kids, but that was three days ago, I was having a bad day. Why can't you just get over it? Keep up!"

Many of my friends live under constant fire through this type of destructive communication, and I can say with certainty that it has crippled their hearts and crushed their spirits.

*****

*The words of a man's mouth are deep waters, but
the fountain of wisdom is a bubbling brook.*
Prov 18.4

Schemes, hidden motives, and duplicity are the deep waters of an untamed tongue. Man's words hold hidden meanings and agendas. They are dark and conceal untold danger, but words of wisdom are apparent, peaceful, and refreshing.

Just ask a poverty stricken child who is given encouragement by the teacher who recognizes his potential. Ask the patient of physical therapy learning to walk again about the power of hopeful words. Think about training children to do, well, anything. Don't we speak words of wisdom and encouragement? "You can do it...good job...keep trying...way to go!"

Which teachers had the greatest impact on your life: the ones who criticized, demeaned, and expressed terrible dissatisfaction with your performance, or the ones who helped you celebrate your successes, great and small? Which friends do you prefer to spend time with: the ones that are condemning of you, or the ones that love and accept you? Think about your job. Are you more inclined to work hard and be productive when your labor is recognized and commended, or when your boss is unappreciative and devalues your effort? Do you think words mean anything? Have they made any difference in your life?

*****

*Pleasant words are a honeycomb, sweet to the
spirit and healing to the bones.* Prov 16.24

When I was in the seventh grade, our family was in the throes of financial hardship, unemployment, and uncertainty. I was stressed by our issues at home and my own personal challenges: a nerd before that was popular, taller than everyone in my class (even some of my teachers), undeveloped, sporting thick owl-eye glasses and a hearing aid that Matt (my husband) jokes about cranking with a recoiling rope pull! I was the poster child for awkward adolescence.

To add to my misery, my best friend from infancy had moved away, leaving a crater the size of the Grand Canyon in my heart. Frequent migraines and bouts of depression required medication with side effects, which made me suicidal. I felt like I was in a tunnel and couldn't see the light of day.

One morning, I woke and found a note on the kitchen table with my name scribbled on it. It was nothing fancy, just written on paper torn out of a spiral bound notebook. My family often left notes for each other in the kitchen, as my parents left for work early and this was before cell phones, voicemail, and email. But never before had a note been just for me.

I wondered if I was in trouble or if it was an important reminder. The note read like this:

Tracie,

I just wanted to take time and tell you how proud I am to have you for my daughter. You are growing up so fast. Before long you will be in high school and then college.

God has given you a talent and I want you to use it for Him. You really have more than one talent, you have many! It is very important that you practice your flute and piano. To do this is to make your talents useful to God.

I am so proud of the way you have your daily devotions. I hope you will always continue to do this. Only reading God's Word can you know God's will for your life. I must get to work. Love, Mom

My eyes fill with tears, remembering the first time I read this letter. Unaware of the depth of my despair but led by the Spirit, my mother wrote the words: "I am proud of you…You have talent…God can use you." They were words of encouragement, hope, LIFE. When I read them, I wept.

That day, I went to school with spirits lifted and a renewed belief that I was loved and accepted. Hope filled me as I trusted that God could someday use even a mess like me!

Through middle school, high school, college, twenty years of marriage and eleven relocations, I have saved this note from Mom. It is permanently creased from the original folds and those impressed from a quarter of a century of preservation.

When I read the words, I am transported back to my childhood dining room table, sitting down for breakfast alone, preparing for another abysmal day at school, but this time, with a sense of hope. The words still speak truth and life to me.

I treasure this letter. I keep it hidden in a box with other keepsakes. And I am left wondering, are my words treasured by others?

*****

Proverbs chapter six begins with a warning for the son not to speak in haste and promise to put up security for a friend's debt. In doing so, he foolishly assumes responsibility for financial risks beyond his control and influence.

If we are afraid to say no or to disappoint someone, we, like the foolish son, entrap ourselves and wear the weight of our words spoken in haste and folly.

Conversation that damages another person, whether it is a neighbor, co-worker, friend, or even our children, can also weigh us down and entangle us when our inconsistencies and hypocrisy are revealed. We can become trapped by our very own words.

Proverbs instructs us and the foolish son to use a direct approach in Prov 6.2-5:

If you have been trapped by what you have said, ensnared by the words of your mouth, then do this my son, to free yourself, since you have fallen into your neighbor's hands: Go and humble yourself; press your plea with your neighbor! Allow no sleep to your eyes, no slumber to your eyelids. Free yourself, like a gazelle from the hand of the hunter, like a bird from the snare of the fowler.

It is simple and direct. Go to them and make amends.

Obviously there may be other conversations we must have with others that also hurt or sting a little but are necessary and beneficial. These are confrontations concerning a personal offense,[18] revealing an area of sin with the motive of repentance and restoration,[19] or promoting peace and unity, wisely teaching and admonishing one another[20] in the name of Christ. All of these are to be approached not from selfish ambition or vain conceit but in humility and consideration of another's best interest.²¹

However, when our words have fractured, crushed, or ruined another, we are to go and ask forgiveness for the harm we have done. Don't wait. Otherwise, we begin to feel stuck. You know what I am talking about; it's that heavy feeling that something isn't right, that someone has been hurt by your words, and now there is something between you. Humble yourself and earnestly ask, "Will you forgive me?"

*****

Crowning Wisdom

Society today has diminished the consequences of words. In a world of texting, posting, and blogging; chat rooms, gossip columns, and heated online debates; with false accusations, fabricated stories, and exaggerated truth, we continue to devalue the power of words.

It is easy to issue a retraction and apology, but the damage remains. A false accusation of inappropriate conduct haunts the accused for the rest of his life like a dark cloud. How do we redirect the next generation? How do we reinforce the power of words and the impact it makes to the world around them? How do we recapture and respect a tool that is powerful enough to pierce like a double-edged sword or heal like an ever-blooming tree of life?

Proverbs beautifully contrasts the mouth of the righteous vs. the mouth of the wicked, words of a fool vs. words of the wise, and the consequences of speaking life vs. speaking words that bring ruin.

You will also find warnings against speaking rashly, caution against airing your own opinions, and explanations for how gossip ruins friendships.

Proverbs persuades us to guard our tongue, *weigh our words,* and keep watch over what we say. In doing so, we will find that our speech no longer crushes another's soul or pierces like a sword but brings health and healing to hungry hearts.

Tongue & Speech

- Prov 4.24 *Put away perversity from your mouth; keep corrupt talk far from your lips.*

- Prov 12.13 *An evil man is trapped by his sinful talk, but a righteous man escapes trouble.*

- Prov 15.1 *A gentle answer deflects anger, but harsh words make tempers flare.*[1]

- Prov 25.11 *A word aptly spoken is like apples of gold in settings of silver.*

- Prov 27.2 *Let another praise you and not your own mouth; someone else and not your own lips.*

False Testimony & Lies

- Prov 14.25 *A truthful witness saves lives but a false witness is deceitful.*

- Prov 24.26 *An honest answer is like a kiss of friendship.*[1]

- Prov 26.28 *A lying tongue hates those it hurts, and a flattering mouth works ruin.*

Gossip

- Prov 11.13 *A gossip betrays a confidence, but a trustworthy man keeps a secret.*

- Prov 17.9 *He who covers an offense promotes love, but whoever repeats the matter separates close friends.*

- Prov 18.8 *Rumors are dainty morsels that sink deep into one's heart.*[1]

- Prov 20.19 *A gossip betrays a confidence; so avoid a man who talks too much.*

- Prov 26.20 *Without wood a fire goes out; without gossip a quarrel dies down.*

Words of the Wise vs. Speech of Fools

- Prov 10.19 *When words are many, sin is not absent, but he who holds his tongue is wise.*

- Prov 14.3 *A fool's talk brings a rod to his back, but the lips of the wise protect them.*

- Prov 17.28 *Even a fool is thought wise if he keeps silent, and discerning if he holds his tongue.*

- Prov 18.2 *A fool finds no pleasure in understanding but delights in airing his own opinions.*

- Prov 17.27 *A man of knowledge uses words with restraint, and a man of understanding is even tempered.*

- Prov 25.24 *Better to live on a corner of the roof than share a house with a quarrelsome wife.*

- Prov 18.13 *He who answers before listening—that is his folly and his shame.*

Chapter Nine

WARNING! "CANCEL THE FIRE TRUCKS"

Have you ever noticed that today drug manufacturers take three to four pages in a magazine to advertise one single drug? The first usually pictures a remarkably healthy looking "patient" whose life has been improved by use of said drug, but the remaining advertisement contains warnings, cautions, contraindications, drug interactions, and so forth?

Do you ever read those warnings? Does anyone? Sure, we may read how this drug will make our symptoms go away, but we don't like to read that this new eye drop may cause some rather unpleasant side effects such as growth of a new appendage, dental itching, death, or worse!

What about these other commonly observed or repeated warnings:

- "Do not swim alone."
- "Don't talk to strangers."
- "Look both ways before crossing the street."
- "Don't drink and drive."

Some warnings are a little absurd or unproven:

- "Wait 30 minutes after eating to go swimming." (Even though this is unproven, I still feel like a terrible mother if I break this "rule.")
- "Caution: Ice cream is cold." (Ha ha, really?)
- "Caution: Coffee is hot." (You don't say!)
- Baby Lotion: "Keep away from children." (Huh?)

- Hairdryer: "Do not use while bathing." (Why would I?)
- Clothing Iron: "Never iron clothes on body." (Okay, now you're making me feel like an idiot.)
- Chainsaw: "Do not attempt to stop chain with hands." (Wow, you really do think I am an idiot, don't you?)

How about more humorous warning labels such as those present on children's toys:

- Warning: "This bag is not a toy."
- Interactive Toy Duck Launch and Load®: "Keep fingers and eyes away from moving wings....tell others you are playing with Interactive Toy Duck Launch and Load." (Am I to announce to the world, "I'm going to launch my toy duck now? Fore!)
- Toy Broom: "This broom does not fly." (Bummer, I was hoping to spy ol' Nessie on my way over to Hogwarts!)

Some of these warnings should go without saying. It should be quite obvious to anyone that a tiny inflatable toy is not a life-saving device, that a peanut granola bar contains peanuts, and that a Halloween cape does not enable its user to fly.

The problem is that in Western culture, we seem to have lost the ability to carefully weigh the consequences of our actions. We aren't quite as wise or don't have the common sense of the previous generations. Even so, we certainly don't seem to like warnings very much.

How many of us truly obey the speed limit 100% of the time?

In spite of the increased incidence of automobile accidents caused by talking on cell phones, operating iPods, GPS devices, texting, and using other techno gadgets, how many of us actually respond to those warnings with a commitment to cease using them entirely while operating a vehicle?

What about smoking? Aren't the labels large enough? Isn't the evidence of its harm to our bodies conclusive?

Remember the old "just say no" commercials and the fried egg? "This is your brain (egg) and this is your brain on drugs" (cracked egg fries in hot pan). Do warnings really work? The obvious answer is not unless you heed them.

*****

Disclaimer: The following content is very Southern, and may be potentially offensive to those with heightened grammatical sensibilities. Consider yourselves warned!

Long, long ago, in a duplex far, far away, my loving husband decided to surprise me by fixing dinner. We had grown tired of baked chicken, grilled chicken, chicken casserole, chicken and dumplings, chicken a la king, chicken salad, BBQ chicken, chicken sandwiches, and steak-fried chicken.

If you are not from the South and have no idea what steak-fried chicken is, I can't help you. We don't actually know what it is either, but it is go-od!

He got a wild hair and decided to fry up some Salisbury Steaks. Problem is, he also decided to dub a few tapes on the stereo in the process.

For you fetuses reading this story, that was the equivalent of ripping a song from one tape and recording it onto another. It was the best way to create our own playlist with a tape, which we called a "mix."

I know, not a trendy term, but we didn't feel the need to brand every new idea and concept until the iGeneration came along!

The first sign of trouble was that he had to call and ask me how to fry something. I told him, "Put oil in the pan, turn it on, and throw your meat in."

"Simple 'nuff." He's Canadian, but only by birth. His southern drawl is so convincing that his momma ain't even sure anymore.

Seeing that a good southern fried dinner is not accomplished by meat alone, we had to have its customary carbohydrate companion, 'taters. Ya'll didn't realize I grew up talking like this, did you? Stay with me, I'm taking you the long way home.

Anyway, a good southern meal of Salisbury Steak deserved a heaping helping of mashed potatoes. So hubby added a third task to his culinary agenda. He had to peel real potatoes!

By the second time he called, I figured out that he was trying to make me dinner and that I had better be real clear on how to not char our food, or kitchen for that matter.

I warned him, "Don't get the oil too hot!" "Be careful when you put the meat in, it might splatter." "The potatoes have to boil for a while or they won't mash." All the while, I heard the familiar sound of Southern Gospel music blaring in the background.

Now, you don't have to be a rocket scientist to see where I'm heading with this story...

By this time, I was getting close to home. I enjoyed the hour long commute from college every afternoon as I listened to music, thought about classes, and calculated how little homework I could get by with while maintaining decent grades. Shoot, I was just aiming for passing grades at this point.

When I pulled in, my own music was so loud, I didn't hear the fire truck pulling in right behind me. I just sat there singing at the top of my lungs, and because I am OCD, I can't just stop in the middle of a song. I need closure, people!

Matt stood indoors at the window next to my car, beating on it furiously to warn me not to come in, but of course I couldn't see or hear him as I was finishing my aria.

When I finally looked up and saw the fire truck, my initial thought was that something happened next door to us, but once I saw the firefighters rushing through my own front door, I jumped out and chased after them!

I rushed in to get the cat, much to the firemen's shock and dismay, and then I saw Matt walking around the front corner of the house.

He had wide eyes and looked perturbed that I had not only ignored his signals from the window but had also entered the home because I was concerned about the cat!

I asked him what happened as if I couldn't have guessed.

He proceeded to tell me that everything was fine, he was not hurt, but we might not get our deposit back on our lease.

"And we need a new rug," he added.

*****

After our last call, he realized that I would be home soon and tried to cook the food faster. Ignoring the warnings about overheating the oil, he not only turned the burner on high, but also put a lid on it for good measure.

With the water boiling next to the frying pan, he turned from the stove to peel the potatoes, while periodically running back and forth to the stereo.

In a matter of minutes, he heard a loud, "BOOM!" and hit the deck!

He literally dropped to the floor! The lid was blown clean off the pan and flames were shooting out from beneath it with surprising fury. It didn't take long for my beautiful country life calendar, carefully hung beside that very burner, to ignite with impressive expediency.

Once the blaze ascended the wall, he decided it might be a good idea to call 911.

While talking to the dispatcher, he searched around for something to smother the fire with. I thank God above he had sense enough not to douse it in water.

He grabbed the only thing he could think of that wasn't flammable.

I must admit now, this revealed some quick thinking on his part. He remembered that the rug by our back door had rubber backing to keep it from slipping.

He picked up the entire rug, while still talking to the 911 Operator, of course, because they won't let you off the phone in the middle of a bonafide emergency.

He began to awkwardly swat at the flames and smother them as best he could with a stiff two by three swath of carpet in one hand and a cordless brick of a phone in the other.

By this time the 911 Communications Officer informed him that the firemen were on their way and he must exit the premises immediately. He kindly explained that he was "taking care of it" and would like to cancel the fire trucks. But she yelled at him and insisted he evacuate.

By this time, I pulled in. Singing my songs, I paid no attention to his frantic efforts to signal me from the living room window.

As the fire truck pulled in, he opened the door to welcome the rushed firemen and apologized profusely for this gross display of culinary ineptitude.

Swept up in the rush to the kitchen, he exited the back door as I entered the front, looking for Sweet Pea, our skittish cat.

Finally, the firemen forced me out and began assessing the damage. They brought in industrial sized fans to blow out the smoke and then lectured him on the dangers of cooking and me on the dangers of hanging ugly calendars by the stove.

Once they departed, we stood in the yard laughing. After all was said and done, it was a night we wouldn't forget!

We surveyed the damage and determined that as far as the food was concerned, it was a total loss.

The kitchen, however, only suffered smoke damage, minor burns, one melted overhead microwave fan, and a highly distressed doormat.

Sweet Pea couldn't have cared less. However, she was a peculiar cat and was known for barking like a dog on occasion and accused of being possessed more often than I care to admit. You just can't judge by her.

Hungry and deflated by his efforts at surprising me with a new dish for dinner, we headed to the local Cracker Barrel for a glass of cold sweet tea and a plate of good ol' southern cooking. Steak-fried chicken.

*****

Crowning Wisdom

That story has nothing to do with Proverbs, but it has a little to do with heeding a warning.

Proverbs has quite a few warnings for the individual wise enough to listen. As a matter of fact, Proverbs has a name for the person unwilling to heed a warning: a fool. Sometimes he is also called the mocker or scoffer. Proverbs 9.12 warns, *If you are wise, your wisdom will reward you, if you are a mocker, you alone will suffer.*

I wonder that with all of the warnings we see daily, the godly counsel from a mature believer, and God's warnings to us in Scripture, do we recognize true wisdom when we hear it? Do we even care?

A Strong Warning Against Adultery

- Prov 5

> 1-6 *My son, pay attention to my wisdom, listen well to my words of insight. That you may maintain discretion and your lips may preserve knowledge. For the lips of an adulteress drip honey, and her speech is smoother than oil; but in the end she is bitter as gall, sharp as a double-edged*

sword. Her feet go down to death; her steps lead straight to the grave. She gives no thought to the way of life; her paths are crooked, but she knows it not.

7-14 *Now then, my sons, listen to me; do not turn aside from what I say. Keep to a path far from her, do not go near the door of her house, lest you give your best strength to others and your years to one who is cruel, lest strangers feast on your wealth and your toil enrich another man's house. At the end of your life you will groan, when your flesh and body are spent. You will say, "How I hated discipline! How my heart spurned correction! I would not obey my teachers or listen to my instructors. I have come to the brink of utter ruin in the midst of the whole assembly."*

15-19 *Drink water from your own cistern, running water from your own well. Should your springs overflow in the streets, your streams of water in the public squares? Let them be yours alone, never to be shared with strangers. May your fountain be blessed, and may you rejoice in the wife of your youth. A loving doe, a graceful deer—may her breasts satisfy you always, may you ever be captivated by her love.*

20-23 *Why be captivated, my son, by an adulteress? Why embrace the bosom of another man's wife? For man's ways are in full view of the Lord, and he examines all his paths. The evil deeds of a wicked man ensnare him; the cords of his sin hold him fast. He will die for lack of discipline, led astray by his own great folly.*

- Prov 23.26-28 *My son, give me your heart and let your eyes keep to my ways, for a prostitute is a deep pit and a wayward* wife is a narrow well. Like a bandit she lies in wait, and multiplies the unfaithful among men.

- Additional passages on the Adulteress can be found in Proverbs 6.20-35 and Proverbs 7.

BUSINESS & FRAUD

- Prov 20.17 *Food gained by fraud tastes sweet to a man, but he ends up with a mouth full of gravel.*
- Prov 21.6 *A fortune made by a lying tongue is a fleeting vapor and a deadly snare.*
- Prov 22.26-27 *Do not be a man who strikes hands in pledge or puts up security for debts; if you lack the means to pay, your very bed will be snatched out from under you.*
- Prov 28.20 *A faithful man will be richly blessed, but one eager to get rich will not go unpunished.*

DRUNKENNESS

- Prov 23.19-21 *Listen, my son and keep your heart on the right path. Do not join those who drink too much wine or gorge themselves on meat, for drunkards and gluttons become poor and drowsiness clothes them in rags.*
- Prov 23.29-35 *Who has woe? Who has sorrow? Who has strife? Who has complaints? Who has needless bruises? Who has bloodshot eyes? Those who linger over wine, who go to sample bowls of mixed wine. Do not gaze at wine when it is red, when it sparkles in the cup, when it goes down smoothly! In the end it bites like a snake and poisons like a viper. Your eyes will see strange sights and your mind imagine confusing things. You will*

be like one sleeping on the high seas, lying on top of the rigging. "They hit me," you will say, "but I'm not hurt! They beat me, but I don't feel it! When will I wake up so I can find another drink?"

Enticement
- Prov 1.10-19

10 *My son, if sinners entice you, do not give in to them.*

11 *If they say, "Come along with us; let's lie in wait for someone's blood, lets waylay some harmless soul;*

12 *let's swallow them alive like the grave, and whole, like those who go down to the pit;*

13 *we will get all sorts of valuable things and fill our houses with plunder;*

14 *throw in your lot with us, and we will share a common purse"—*

15 *my son, do not go along with them, do not set foot on their paths;*

16 *for their feet rush into sin, they are swift to shed blood.*

17 *How useless to spread a net in full view of all the birds!*

18 *These men lie in wait for their own blood; they waylay only themselves!*

19 *Such is the end of all who go after ill-gotten gain; it takes away the lives of those who get it."*

- Prov 9.13-18

    13 *The woman Folly is loud; she is undisciplined and without knowledge.*

    14 *She sits at the door of her house, on a seat at the highest point of the city,*

    15 *calling out to those who pass by, who go straight on their way.*

    16 *"Let all who are simple come in here!" she says to those who lack judgment.*

    17 *"Stolen water is sweet; food eaten in secret is delicious!"*

    18 *But little do they know that the dead are there, that her guests are in the depths of the grave.*

Fools & their Folly

- Prov 12.15 *The way of a fool seems right to him, but a wise man listens to advice.*

- Prov 12.16 *A fool shows his annoyance at once, but a prudent man overlooks insult.*

- Prov 13.20 *Walk in the wise and become wise, for a companion of fools suffers harm.*

- Prov 14.18 *The simple inherit folly, but the prudent are crowned with knowledge.*

- Prov 23.9 *Do not speak to a fool, for he will scorn the wisdom of your words.*

- Prov 26.1-12

    1 *Like* snow in summer, or rain in harvest, honor is not fitting for a fool.

    2 *Like* a fluttering sparrow or a darting swallow, an undeserved curse does not come to rest.

    3 A whip for the horse, a halter for the donkey, and a rod for the backs of fools!

    4 Do not answer a fool according to his folly, or you will be *like* him yourself.

    5 Answer a fool according to his folly, or he will be wise in his own eyes.

    6 *Like* cutting off one's feet or drinking violence is the sending of a message by the hand of a fool.

    7 *Like* a lame man's legs that hang limp is a proverb in the mouth of a fool.

    8 *Like* tying a stone in a sling is the giving of honor to a fool.

    9 *Like* a thornbush in a drunkard's hand is a proverb in the mouth of a fool.

    10 *Like* an archer who wounds at random is he who hires a fool or any passer-by.

    11 As a dog returns to its vomit, so a fool repeats his folly.

    12 Do you see a man wise in his own eyes? There is more hope for a fool than for him.

- Prov 28.26 He who trusts in himself is a fool, but he who walks in wisdom is kept safe.

- Prov 30.32-33 *If you have played the fool and exalted yourself, or if you have planned evil, clap your hand over your mouth! For as churning the milk produces butter, and as twisting the nose produces blood, so stirring up anger produces strife.*

Greed & Envy

- Prov 14.30 *A heart at peace gives life to the body, but envy rots the bones.*

- Prov 15.27 *A greedy man brings trouble to his family, but he who hates bribes will live.*

- Prov 23.1-3 *When you sit to dine with a ruler, note well what is before you, and put a knife to your throat if you are given to gluttony. Do not crave his delicacies, for that food is deceptive.*

- Prov 23.4-5 *Do not wear yourself out to get rich; have the wisdom to show restraint. Cast but a glance at riches, and they are gone, for they will surely sprout wings and fly off to the sky like an eagle.*

- Prov 28.25 *A greedy man stirs up dissension, but he who trusts in the Lord will prosper.*

Indulgence

- Prov 28.7 *He who keeps the law is a discerning son, but a companion of gluttons disgraces his father.*

- Prov 29.21 *If a man pampers his servant from youth, he will bring grief in the end.*

PRIDE

- Prov 11.2 *When pride comes, then comes disgrace, but with humility comes wisdom.*

- Prov 16.18 *Pride goes before destruction, a haughty spirit before a fall.*

- Prov 27.21 *The crucible for silver and the furnace for gold, but man is tested by the praise he receives.*

- Prov 29.23 *A man's pride brings him low, but a man of lowly spirit gains honor.*

RUIN & CONSEQUENCES OF DECEPTION

- Prov 11.17 *A kind man benefits himself, but a cruel man brings trouble on himself.*

- Prov 11.27 *He who seeks good finds good will, but evil comes to him who searches for it.*

- Prov 17.13 *If a man pays back evil for good, evil will never leave his house.*

- Prov 26.27 *If a man digs a pit, he will fall into it; if a man rolls a stone, it will roll back on him.*

- Prov 29.6 *An evil man is snared by his own sin, but a righteous one can sing and be glad.*

THE STINGY MAN

- Prov 23.6-8 *Don't eat with people who are stingy; don't desire their delicacies. They are always thinking about how much it costs. "Eat and drink," they say, but they don't mean it. You will throw up what little you've eaten, and your compliments will be wasted.*[1]

- Prov 28.22 *A stingy man is eager to get rich and is unaware that poverty awaits him.*

Chapter Ten

WEALTH & RESOURCES: FRUIT LOOPS & WINE

This is to my Father's glory, that you bear much fruit, showing yourselves to be my disciples.
John 15.8

In the parable of the talents, Jesus told a story of a master who went on a journey and entrusted varying amounts of wealth to his servants to use in his stead. Upon the master's return, the servants who invested and used the resources to produce a profit for their master were praised and given more to manage. One servant had no use for the master's talent and buried it, producing nothing for the master. He was rebuked and cast out, seemingly condemned to hell.[22]

In the Bible, many passages instruct us to be productive.

God blessed Adam and Eve and told them, *Be fruitful and increase in number.*[23]

He speaks of fruits of the Spirit in Galatians 5.22-23. The attributes listed are evidence (yield, fruit, products) of the presence of His Spirit in our lives.

The Righteous are characterized as trees bearing (producing) good fruit, whereas those that do not are *cut down and thrown into the fire.*[24]

Jesus described himself as the vine, urging his followers to abide in him, to remain in him, so that they would be fruitful, producing a harvest. He warned that God the Father is the Gardener and cuts off those who do not bear fruit.[25]

Jesus also cursed a fig tree in leaf that bore no actual fruit.[26]

I don't know about you, but I sense that God wants us to be fruitful and productive. Yet, it is not for the sake of appearances, for selfish gain, or even for our salvation. It is for His glory.

*****

Honor the Lord with your wealth, with the firstfruits of all your crops. Prov 3.9

I have known Jake and Sarah for years, and have been privileged to watch God do extraordinary things in their lives. They were high school sweethearts and have been together since their sophomore year, which is in itself remarkable.

Jake and Sarah seem to have a mindset for creating wealth, as evidenced by their work ethic and the tireless pursuit of creative ways to generate income. They have found value in using every possible interest, skill, and connection as a potential source of revenue.

In addition to Jake's full time job, both have created small businesses in graphic design, printing, website development, and other artistic ventures. Working together, they utilize strengths they have both individually and collectively, maximizing their chances for success. They are productive.

Early in their marriage, Jake and Sarah did not see money as a resource to be used by God and for His kingdom. They saw it as a tool to get the things they wanted and needed. They operated in an endless cycle of supply and demand: the greater their resources, the greater their demand for new material goods.

The fruit of their labors continually returned back to serve their own purposes, needs, and wants. It was a vicious cycle that many struggle to break free of today.

Through a church small group study, they completed a Bible-based financial class, which taught godly stewardship of wealth and resources.

In it, they were challenged to rethink everything they believed about work, wealth, talent, and time. They were first challenged to give God a tithe, or tenth, of their earnings. It was the "first" fruits of their labor: their first and best. Firstfruits.

This was difficult, and it hurt a little. It involved forfeiting some of the things they believed they wanted and should have. However, in making those sacrifices, they quickly learned that they actually needed less and wanted less.

Jake and Sarah trusted God's promise that follows the command to honor God with your wealth: *then your barns will be filled to overflowing and your vats will brim over with new wine.* Prov 3.10

However, it was not overnight that their barns were filled to overflowing. It took planning, hard work, and patience as we read about in Prov 21.5, *The plans of the diligent lead to profit, as surely as haste leads to poverty.*

Not every new venture was rewarding, and not every success was overwhelming. But they were diligent, patient, and trusted God to bless the fruit of their labor, great and small.

*****

*One man pretends to be rich, yet has nothing;
another pretends to be poor, yet has great wealth.*
Prov 13.7

There began a transformation for Jake and Sarah from a mindset of ownership to that of stewardship. God had emphasized this to the Israelites in the observance of the Sabbath Year and the Year of Jubilee, telling them, *the land is mine and you are but aliens and my tenants.*[27]

Likewise, Jake and Sarah began to view everything they had as belonging to God, the master. Their home, work, income, and time were all His, to be used for Him and His glory.

As they continued to assess their finances and see their income grow, it became clear that outstanding debt was limiting their ability to do more for God and His kingdom. God was prompting their hearts toward service to others, opening their eyes to the needy, and growing in them a desire to help finance missions and those doing mission work.

But they had to face their debt head on. No longer was it their money, but God's money, and His money was paying for interest and excesses they no longer needed or desired.

Isn't pretending to be rich the American way? When we live on credit and amass things to make our lives more comfortable, we live like kings. However, we become spiritually bankrupt as the weight of those excesses often enslave us, isolate us from our faith community, and rob us of peace.

Jake and Sarah recognized that they were pretending to be rich and decided to discipline themselves to begin living poorly.

This was another difficult step, as it required discipline and commitment. By trading in their high dollar SUV, establishing a budget, cutting back on dining out, and spending only from cash reserves, they were able to pay more on their debt.

Trusting that God would honor their efforts, they continued in this direction and saw their debt melt away, along with the burden and limitations it imposed.

They were no longer enslaved, but free: delivered from debt, worry, and superficial desires. They had been liberated and set free to tithe consistently, offer their time and talents, give generously to those in need, and financially support missions for the kingdom.

*****

Commit to the Lord whatever you do and your plans will succeed. Prov 16.3

Life, however, takes unexpected turns. Poor business decisions and mismanagement by employers put Jake into a precarious position. Faced with riding out the storm or taking a greater risk to branch out in a new opportunity, Jake prayerfully chose to branch out and trusted God to provide.

At the same time, Jake and Sarah conceived an idea for a new personal business venture that could possibly generate income while providing a creative outlet for their graphic and technological interests. Did I mention that they are highly productive people?

They pursued this new concept as a possible safety net, trusting that their diligence and hard work would yield a harvest. Committing this business venture to God, they prayed for His blessings and guidance through the process.

It fit a niche that few had noticed before. Working tirelessly at both jobs, not knowing which would be successful, they poured their collective energy and creativity into this idea, and God did bless their efforts. Their barns began to fill to overflowing and their vats to brim over with new wine!

*****

He who pursues righteousness and love, finds life, prosperity, and honor. Prov 21.21

As they have experienced spiritual and financial growth, they have grown in their giving. A tithe no longer feels like enough! After all, their needs have not significantly increased and their wants have long been redefined. Jake and Sarah are thrilled to participate in God's mission and seek opportunities to bless others. Through all of this, God gets the glory.

Today, Jake and Sarah continue working their business, serving and leading in their local church in Huntersville, North Carolina, and they faithfully leverage every possible asset they possess for God's use.

God has multiplied their "talents" as a result of their faithfulness. As they have pursued wisdom in their finances, carefully stewarding everything He has granted them, they have received blessings both financially and spiritually. A new cycle has begun!

It honors God when we are resourceful and productive with what He has given us!

Scripture emphasizes that He wants us to be fruitful and productive in all areas of our lives. We are called to have fruitful spiritual lives, fruitful relationships, and to be fruitful with our time, resources, and our work.

It is a righteous pursuit to honor God, the Lord of the Harvest, our Master, and through our productivity, see Him glorified.

*****

Crowning Wisdom

Proverbs offers wisdom on matters of wealth and resources. It cautions us against placing our hope in riches, counsels against attitudes that make us unproductive and selfish, and warns about unfair business practices. It promotes the diligent and hard worker, the compassionate, and seekers of righteousness.

Godly wisdom challenges us to rethink our source and responsibility of material wealth. It reveals that the greatest treasures we can pursue in life are the wisdom, knowledge, and understanding of God. In that, He is glorified and we are blessed beyond riches.

RICH MAN & POOR MAN

- Prov 14.23 *All hard work brings a profit, but mere talk leads only to poverty.*

- Prov 19.17 *He who is kind to the poor lends to the Lord, and he will reward him for what he has done.*

- Prov 21.5 *The plans of the diligent lead to profit, as surely as haste leads to poverty.*

- Prov 21.6 *A fortune made by a lying tongue is a fleeting vapor and a deadly snare.*

- Prov 28.19 *He who works his land will have abundant food, but the one who chases fantasies will have his fill of poverty.*

WEALTH & RESOURCES

- Prov 11.24 *One man gives freely, yet gains even more; another withholds unduly but comes to poverty.*

- Prov 11.25 *A generous man will prosper, he who refreshes others will himself be refreshed.*

- Prov 13.11 *Dishonest money dwindles away, but he who gathers money little by little makes it grow.*

- Prov 15.16 *Better a little with the fear of the Lord than great wealth with turmoil.*

- Prov 30. 7-9 *Two things I ask of you, O Lord; do not refuse me before I die: Keep falsehood and lies far from me; give me neither poverty nor riches, but give me only my daily bread. Otherwise, I may have too much and disown you and say, "Who is the Lord?" Or I may become poor and steal, and so dishonor the name of my God.*

Chapter Eleven

WISDOM: "THE FOOL DOTH THINK HE WISE"

If you simply enter the word "wisdom" in any search engine on the internet, you will find countless websites dedicated to the collection of "wise" sayings. You will find quotes from notable authors, inventors, politicians, great thinkers, religious figures, leaders, and the list goes on.

These words of "wisdom" tend to eloquently express a truth they have observed in life or an insight into the interplay between our words, actions, thoughts, and human nature.

What I find very interesting is that many of the quotes that we have heard from these notable people have underlying origins in Scripture.

"It is better to remain silent at the risk of being thought a fool, than to talk and remove all doubt of it." –Maurice Switzer

Even a fool is though wise if he keeps silent, and discerning if he holds his tongue. Prov 17.28

The heart of fools blurt out folly. Prov 12.23b

"Try not to become a man of success. Rather become a man of value." –Albert Einstein

A good name is more desirable than great riches; to be esteemed is better than silver or gold. Prov 22.1

"Before you embark on a journey of revenge, dig two graves." –Confucius

If a man digs a pit, he will fall into it; if a man rolls a stone, it will roll back on him. Prov 26.27

"Angry people are not always wise." –Jane Austen, *Pride and Prejudice*

A fool gives full vent to his anger, but a wise man keeps himself under control. Prov 29.11

"The fool doth think he is wise, but the wise man knows himself to be a fool." –William Shakespeare, *As You Like It*

Do not be wise in your own eyes. Prov 3.7a

Do you see a man wise in his own eyes? There is more hope for a fool than for him. Prov 26.12

Other common sayings:

"Behind every great man is a great woman."

A wife of noble character who can find? She is worth far more than rubies. Her husband has full confidence in her and lacks nothing of value. She brings him good, not harm, all the days of her life. Prov 31.10-12

Her husband is respected at the city gate, where he takes his seat among the elders of the land. Prov 31.23 *And he praises her, "Many women do noble things, but you surpass them all."* Prov 31.28b-29

"Don't bite the hand that feeds you!"

A king's wrath is like the roar of a lion; he who angers him forfeits his life. Prov 20.2

"He's not the sharpest tool in the shed."

Using a dull ax requires great strength, so sharpen the blade. That's the value of wisdom; it helps you succeed. Ecclesiastes 10:10

"Make hay while the sun shines." –John Heywood

Go to the ant you sluggard; consider its ways and be wise! It has no commander, no overseer or ruler, yet it stores its provisions in summer and gathers its food at harvest. Prov 6.6-8

This is not to say that these people were unoriginal, but rather, God established true wisdom. *The Lord brought me forth as the first of his works, before his deeds of old; I [Wisdom] was appointed from eternity, from the beginning, before the world began.*[28]

*****

Inspired Wisdom was extraordinary and evident through the life of King Solomon. He is regarded as the wisest man to have ever lived, besides Jesus Christ Himself, and the passage below explains why this is true, even today:

God gave Solomon wisdom and very great insight, and a breadth of understanding as measureless as the sand on the seashore. Solomon's wisdom was greater than the wisdom of all the men of the East, and greater than all the wisdom of Egypt. He was wiser than any other man, including Ethan the Ezrahite—wiser than Heman, Calcol and Darda, the sons of Mahol. And his fame spread to all the surrounding nations. He spoke three thousand proverbs and his songs numbered a thousand and five. He described plant life, from the cedar of Lebanon to the hyssop that grows out of walls. He also taught about animals and birds, reptiles and fish. Men of all nations came to listen to Solomon's wisdom, sent by all the kings of the world, who had heard of his wisdom. I Kings 4.29-34[1]

Solomon was the son and successor of King David of Israel. King Solomon was greatly influenced by his father's love and devotion to the God of Israel and *showed his love for the Lord by walking according to the statutes of his father David.*[29] He worshipped the Lord with great dedication and unparalleled extravagance as Scripture records that he once offered a thousand burnt offerings on the altar at Gibeon.

Later that night at Gibeon, Solomon had a dream where God spoke to him and told him, *Ask for whatever you want me to give you.*[30] Solomon's response was astonishing.

Solomon replied, "You showed faithful love to your servant my father, David, because he was honest and true and faithful to you. And you have continued your faithful love to him today by giving him a son to sit on his throne.

Now, O Lord my God, you have made me king instead of my father, David, but I am like a little child who doesn't know his way around. And here I am in the midst of your own chosen people, a nation so great and numerous they cannot be counted! Give me an understanding heart so that

I can govern your people well and know the difference between right and wrong. For who by himself is able to govern this great people of yours?"

The Lord was pleased that Solomon had asked for wisdom. So God replied, "Because you have asked for wisdom in governing my people with justice and have not asked for a long life or wealth or the death of your enemies—I will give you what you asked for! I will give you a wise and understanding heart such as no one else has had or ever will have! And I will also give you what you did not ask for—riches and fame! No other king in all the world will be compared to you for the rest of your life! And if you follow me and obey my decrees and my commands as your father, David, did, I will give you a long life."

Then Solomon woke up and realized it had been a dream. He returned to Jerusalem and stood before the Ark of the Lord's Covenant, where he sacrificed burnt offerings and peace offerings. Then he invited all his officials to a great banquet. I Kings 3.6-15[1]

This dream was a divine encounter with God. Solomon expressed with humility and sincerity his desire for help and discernment in governing God's people. He demonstrated wisdom from the start in recognizing his incompetence and lack of discernment for such a high calling.

It took wisdom to ask for wisdom.

*****

When all Israel heard the king's decision, the people were in awe of the king, for they saw the wisdom God had given him for rendering justice.
I Kings 3.28[1]

God's promise to Solomon was confirmed by an epic story of two mothers claiming the same young infant as their own.

They were prostitutes that shared a home and both had given birth within days of one another, but one of the infants died as his mother rolled over him in the night. Upon discovering this, she switched her dead son with the live infant from the other mother that same night.

When the other mother woke the next morning to find a dead infant in her bed, she realized that it was not the son she bore. She confronted the other prostitute who denied any wrongdoing.

As their matter was brought before King Solomon, he heard them argue with one another. There were no birth certificates, no medical or diagnostic tests to authenticate either woman's claim to the child. Since they were prostitutes, it would be impossible to have another corroborate either's claim. He needed incredible wisdom for this judgment!

Solomon grew weary of their endless accusations, so he ordered officials to cut the child in two so that each mother could have half! (I'm not making this up!)

Such an appalling judgment revealed the true mother as evidenced by their responses.

One mother cried out to give the child to the other mother. However, the second mother said, go ahead, *neither one of us will have him, cut the child!*

Solomon surmised that the true mother of that child would rather see him live, even apart from her, than to see him perish. He ordered the child to be returned to his rightful mother.

As news of this verdict reached the kingdom, people were amazed at the wisdom Solomon showed in the face of such difficult matters.

*****

The report I heard in my own country about your achievements and your wisdom is true.
-Queen of Sheba

God was with Solomon. He granted him wisdom beyond anyone who had ever lived and would ever live. Kings and nobility traveled great distances to meet the man whose reputation for wisdom and wealth had surpassed them all.

The Queen of Sheba visited Solomon and concluded, *I did not believe these things until I came and saw with my own eyes. Indeed, not even half was told me; in wisdom and wealth you have far exceeded the report I heard…Praise be to the Lord your God, who has delighted in you and placed you on the throne of Israel.*[31]

Solomon's wisdom, knowledge, and wealth remain unsurpassed to this day.

He was brilliant! He recited over three thousand proverbs, composed over one thousand songs, studied and taught others about plant life from the enormous cedars of Lebanon to the small herb-like hyssop that would grow out of walls in the Middle East.

He was also knowledgeable about all types of animals: large beasts, birds, reptiles, fish, and insects. He studied their ways and gained insight into their natural instincts and how it impacted their communities and species.

Solomon would have made Stephen Hawking, Einstein, William James Sidis, even da Vinci appear ordinary. Socrates, Plato, and Aristotle had nothing on Solomon. His wisdom and intelligence were a supernatural gift from God and the whole world knew it!

*****

Crowning Wisdom

Wisdom is a tree of life to those who embrace her; happy are those who hold her tightly. Prov 3.18

Wisdom was to be guardian and guide, an internal compass leading us with truth and clarity and offering hope and life, to those who embrace her.

She grants prudence to the simple and understanding to the foolish. She speaks what is right and true. Her words are just, without being twisted or distorted, and to the discerning ear, they are faultless.

Those seeking Wisdom will find her and find themselves blessed if they keep to her ways.

Solomon, King of Israel, taught his sons, *Blessed is the man who finds wisdom, the man who gains understanding, for she is more profitable than silver and yields better returns than gold.*[32]

Or as Bob Marley put it, "Don't Gain The World and Lose Your Soul, Wisdom Is Better Than Silver Or Gold."

KNOWLEDGE

- Prov 1.7 *The fear of the Lord is the beginning of knowledge, but fools despise wisdom and discipline.*
- Prov 18.15 *The heart of the discerning acquires knowledge; the ears of the wise seek it out.*
- Prov 19.2 *Enthusiasm without knowledge is no good; haste makes mistakes.*[1]
- Prov 23.12 *Apply your heart to instruction and your ears to words of knowledge.*

WISDOM: FINDING THE RIGHT PATH

- Prov 2.1-5 *My son, if you accept my words and store up my commands within you, turning your ear to wisdom and applying your heart to understanding, and if you call out for insight and cry aloud for understanding and if you look for it as for silver and search for it as for hidden treasure, then you will understand the fear of the Lord and find the knowledge of God.*
- Prov 2.6-8 *For the Lord gives wisdom, and from his mouth come knowledge and understanding. He holds victory in store for the upright, he is a shield to those whose walk is blameless, for he guards the course of the just and protects the way of his faithful ones.*
- Prov 2.9-11 *Then you will understand what is right and just and fair—every good path. For wisdom will enter your heart, and knowledge will be pleasant to your soul. Discretion will protect you, and understanding will guard you.*
- Prov 2.12-15 *Wisdom will save you from the ways of wicked men, from men whose words are perverse, who leave the straight*

paths to walk in dark ways, who delight in doing wrong and rejoice in the perverseness of evil, whose paths are crooked and who are devious in their ways.

- Prov 2.16-19 *It will save you also from the adulteress, from the wayward wife with her seductive words, who has left the partner of her youth and ignored the covenant she made before God. For her house leads down to death and her paths to the spirits of the dead. None who go to her return or attain the paths of life.*

- Prov 2.20-22 *Thus you will walk in the ways of good men and keep to the paths of the righteous. For the upright will live in the land, and the blameless will remain in it; but the wicked will be cut off from the land, and the unfaithful will be torn from it.*

- Prov 3.1-2 *My son, do not forget my teaching, but keep my commands in your heart, for they will prolong your life many years and bring you prosperity.*

- Prov 3.3-4 *Let love and faithfulness never leave you; bind them around your neck, write them on the tablet of your heart. They you will win favor and a good name in the sight of God and man.*

- Prov 3.5-6 *Trust in the Lord with all your heart and lean not on your own understanding; in all your ways acknowledge him, and he will make your paths straight.*

- The Blessings of Finding Wisdom are found in Prov 3.13-20
- How Wisdom Protects is found in Prov 3.21-26
- The Supremacy of Wisdom is found in Prov 4.1-27
- Wisdom's Call and Origin is found in Prov 8.1-36
- Wisdom Invites All Who Will Hear in Prov 9.1-12

SOLOMON'S WISDOM ONE LINERS: A SELECTION

- Prov 10.14 *Wise men store up knowledge, but the mouth of a fool invites ruin.*
- Prov 10.19 *When words are many, sin is not absent, but he who holds his tongue is wise.*
- Prov 13.20 *He who walks with the wise grows wise, but a companion of fools suffers harm.*
- Prov 14.8 *The wisdom of the prudent is to give thought to their ways, but the folly of fools is deception.*
- Prov 15.2 *The tongue of the wise commends knowledge, but the mouth of the fool gushes folly.*
- Prov 15.24 *The path of life leads upward for the wise to keep him from going down to the grave.*
- Prov 15.33 *The fear of the Lord teaches a man wisdom, and humility comes before honor.*
- Prov 16.16 *How much better to get wisdom than gold, to choose understanding rather than silver!*
- Prov 17.16 *Of what use is money in the hand of a fool, since he has no desire to get wisdom?*
- Prov 22.3 *A prudent man sees danger and takes refuge, but the simple keep going and suffer for it.*
- Prov 23.9 *Do not speak to a fool, for he will scorn the wisdom of your words.*
- Prov 23.23 *Buy the truth and do not sell it; get wisdom, discipline and understanding.*

- Prov 25.12 *Like an earring of gold or an ornament of fine gold is a wise man's rebuke to a listening ear.*

- Prov 28.11 *A rich man may be wise in his own eyes, but a poor man who has discernment sees through him.*

- Prov 30.2-4 *I am the most ignorant of men; I do not have a man's understanding. I have not learned wisdom, nor have I knowledge of the Holy One. Who has gone up to heaven and come down? Who has gathered up the wind in the hollow of his hands? Who has wrapped up the waters in his cloak? Who has established all the ends of the earth? What is his name, and the name of his son? Tell me if you know!*

Chapter Twelve

WOMEN: MIRACLE BRAS & CHASTITY BELTS

Some of the best feminist rants in a movie, bar none, are through the imagined assassinations of the male chauvinist pig Franklin Hart, Jr. in the 1980 movie *Nine to Five*.

As a child of the eighties, this is one of my favorite movies of all time, and honestly, I still laugh myself silly through it! The three protagonists are mistreated by their "sexist, egotistical, lying, hypocritical, bigot" boss, and in a pot-induced buzz they fantasize about how to "off" their boss. (Parental viewing standards have come a long way!)

As a sinister Snow White alter ego, one dreams of poisoning his coffee and catapulting him right out the window of his high-rise corner office.

The next woman dreams of shooting him execution-style, then mounting his head on the office wall.

The third wishes to give him a taste of his own medicine. She sexually harasses him, and when he resists, a chase ensues where he ends up hogtied and turning on a BBQ spit.

That movie made me aware of the secular work environment where women have fought for recognition, respect, and promotion. Many would claim this was merely Hollywood in exaggerated, over-the-top storytelling, scoffing at the incredulous turn of events, and they would dismiss any correlating reality to these characters' experiences.

However, many women have felt this to be their own experience in the workforce from day one: sexual harassment, explosive bosses, exploitation, devaluation of women's contributions, and a glass ceiling they cannot infiltrate. There is a reason this movie resonated with so many women in eighties.

It has long been accepted that men find their identity through their work, but I suspect that women too have begun to believe that who we are is defined by what we do.

I think it is time we start asking some hard questions. But there is one caveat: answers do us no good if we're asking the wrong questions.

Have you ever asked:

Why do I work hard in school and pursue the degree and career that offers security, wealth, influence, and success? Why do I sacrifice my personal life for my professional life?

Why would I leave my profession to stay home with children, spending my day going from one mess to the next, often feeling each task is menial and mundane? (By the way, Phyllis Diller advised, "Cleaning your house while your kids are still growing is like shoveling the walk before it stops snowing." Just saying...)

Why do I work around the clock on business ventures such as in-home sales, web designs, blogging, or developing that next creative idea?

Why do I need to hover over my children, worrying that they may trip and fall, get abducted, or suffer a bite from a rabid duckling? Why do I heavily guard them from teasing, unfairness, and roughhousing?

Why do I spearhead missional outreaches that provide food to the hungry, shelters for the homeless, educational opportunities and health care to the underserved? Why am I the first to spring into action when disaster strikes or when a need is felt?

These are all good questions, but I believe the "who" should drive the "why." "Who" am I doing all of this for?

However, we must back up further and consider the first half of that question: "Who am I?"

*****

A woman without a man is like a fish without a bicycle. –Gloria Steinem

FEMINISM TODAY

The feminist movement has undoubtedly improved the lifestyle, rights, and opportunities for women today. We stand on the shoulders of our mothers, grandmothers, great-grandmothers, and women who wanted better for us than what they received themselves.

However, what began as a quest for education and equality has morphed into an insatiable drive for autonomy, influence, and power.

The problem is that accomplishments, titles, and independent wealth don't make the person. It makes the image. It's like a miracle bra—we look great in all the right places, but strip that away and we're still just a size A trying to "fake it 'til we make it."

If the underlying question is, "Who am I?" why are we, like men, answering according to our accomplishments and careers? "I am a doctor... professor...writer...an executive...an engineer."

Is that our true identity? Aren't we more than what we do?

Feminism today suggests that if we work hard at our careers, fight for equal rights and opportunities, and prove our worth, we can have it all. We can be in control, we can feel secure, we can stand on our own two feet. We can do anything and we can be anything.

But what if we have been deceived? What if our quest comes at too great of a price? Or worse, what if we now have a case of mistaken identity?

Currently, women in America make more money, work more hours, and sacrifice more than ever. Consequently, we suffer more health problems, broken relationships, and take more medications than ever before.

Sure, we finally have control over our money, our bodies, and our destiny, or so we believe. But, in 2010, Medco Health Solutions reported that one quarter of all American women are on some type of medication to address mental health issues such as depression and anxiety, a rate much higher than men. Others turn to alcohol and substance abuse, while some overeat, declare war on their own bodies, or accept defeat and isolation.

That sounds out of control to me.

Most of us, admittedly, struggle with identity. We are enticed by a feminist culture that tells us we are strong, capable, and do not need a man to give us identity or worth, which at its core, is true.

Feminist culture resists living for and serving another, but always looks to self and self-preservation.

But is feminism the answer? Is that who we really are?

Does living for "me" yield the safeguards of assurance and give me purpose in life? Does it satisfy my soul?

*****

"I'm a server of food and putter on of pants and a bedmaker; somebody who can be called on when you want something. But who am I?" –mother of four, *The Feminine Mystique*, Betty Friedan, 1963

TRADITIONALISM TODAY

Some women embrace a more traditional role maintaining that men and women have different stations and that the ultimate expression of purpose and identity is in childbearing, service to the family, and in subordinate marriages.

Ever hear the phrase, "women belong in the home, barefoot and pregnant?" This is a demeaning and highly offensive phrase used by male chauvinists to reduce a woman's value to that of birthing children and keeping a home.

Women around the world live within social systems that are even more debasing and degrading. Developing countries and non-Christian cultures practice domination of women a variety of ways: withholding education, arranging marriages, denying rights to own property, restricting work outside of the home, and even covering their faces in public.

The woman is not empowered but rather subjugated to the roles and duties dictated by the family head. They are dependent on the patriarch and must function within the confines of a hierarchical system where they are given no voice or influence in the matters and decisions that affect them.

Many world religions embrace this ideology as a vehicle for emphasizing and enforcing the fundamentals of their beliefs.

Even in developed nations, traditional fundamental Christian sects practice a version of these restrictions on women.

This hurts more than it helps—it is cold and religiose, purporting uncompromising righteousness. Like the medieval chastity belts, its appearance alone may ward off "unrighteous" behaviors, but we must tread very lightly or we may get our "knickers" in a knot!

Recognizing that the early church could even be enslaved by over religious and lofty sounding restrictions imposed by human thinking, Paul warned the Colossians that such harsh regulations are actually useless for restraining our sinful desires.

> *You have died with Christ, and he has set you free from the spiritual powers of this world. So why do you keep on following the rules of the world, such as, "Don't handle! Don't taste! Don't touch!"? Such rules are mere human teachings about things that deteriorate as we use them. These rules may seem wise because they require strong devotion, pious self-denial, and severe bodily discipline. But they provide no help in conquering a person's evil desires.* Colossians 2.20-23[1]

Strong devotion. Pious self-denial. Severe bodily discipline. These may make us appear wise, virtuous, even holy, but they ultimately lack the power to transform the heart. Rules and regulations based on human commands and traditions create bondage, whereas Christ sets us free: He brought us to life, forgave our sins, canceled the written code and its former regulations.

Yet, the outcomes in traditionalism may, at times, yield stronger relationships for some, finding satisfaction in clearly defined roles and feeling that a better balance between the sexes has been achieved.

But for others, this approach lacks dignity, feels too restrictive, undermines individuality, and is just as hollow and deceptive as the feminist agenda.

Many women desire greater responsibilities, feel called to explore new interests, or simply seek personal enrichment but are denied these opportunities because they do not fit within the rigid confines of traditionalism.

They are left asking the same questions. "Who am I?" "What is my purpose?"

*****

The feminist's identity is self-determined by her roles and accomplishments. Her purpose is to promote self, independence, and control.

The traditionalist's identity is determined by others: husbands, religious systems, and the social culture. Her purpose is to promote and serve others and meet their needs.

Are we all laboring in vain? Are our souls truly satisfied?

Isaiah invites us to come in our poverty, vanity, and bondage, in our quest for identity and purpose, in our hunger and in our thirst:

Come, all you who are thirsty, come to the waters; and you who have no money, come, buy and eat! Come, buy wine and milk without money and without cost. Why spend your money on what is not bread, and your labor on what does not satisfy? Listen, listen to me, and eat what is good, and your soul will delight in the richest of fare.[33]

What if there is another way? What if the identity we desire is not found in self or in others? What if we could find true satisfaction through relationship instead of roles? What if our purpose extends beyond the confines of our self and our immediate families?

*****

In a wonderful new group study produced by Grace Church in Greenville, South Carolina, the Hebrew word, *Ezer*, is introduced to the modern woman.

In Genesis, after Adam was created, God caused a deep sleep to fall on him. He removed one of the man's ribs, and used it to create woman, his *ezer kenegdo*.

This phrase meaning "suitable helper" or "helper fit" has been commonly reduced to "help meet" or "helper" in most modern texts, but we have failed to adequately convey the full essence of this integral match created for Adam.

An *ezer* was not a servant, was not of lesser intelligence or importance, but an aid, a helper, a strong ally. God refers to Himself as an *ezer* in many contexts and Scriptural passages!

However, *kenegdo* ascribes the essential and incomparable worth of this ally to Adam. "So joined together, *ezer kenegdo* means essential counterpart, indispensable companion, or corresponding strength."[34]

Both Adam and Eve were created in God's image. Nothing else in all creation was designed with features and characteristics innately divine. HE gives us our identity as exclusive bearers of His image!

Although male and female are separate but equal creations, coupled together they reveal a broader view of the fullness of His character and nature.

In essence, God placed within the man characteristics of Himself, some of which may be similar to those found in women, but in larger degree. Likewise, God gave certain characteristics of Himself to women that may be present but not as prevalent in the man. Together, they yield a fuller picture, a composite image capturing greater depth and clarity of the Creator himself.

Single women, widows, and young ladies need not worry that they cannot bear His image outside the context of marriage. Remember, *God created human beings, in his own image. In the image of God he created them; male and female he created them.*[35]

EACH bears His image. EACH bears the expression of His likeness.

Women reflect this image of God to the world through their *ezer* qualities: strength, support, and alliance with others. This is our purpose, our design, our calling in life!

The heart and soul of a woman functions at its maximum capacity within the context of relationships. Not because we find our identity in relationships, but because in relationships, we best reflect His image!

The *Ezer* study has beautifully articulated in greater depth the true identity and purpose given to all women. We are his creation, bearers of His image, expressions of His likeness, purposed with reflecting His nature and character to the created world!

*****

Crowning Wisdom

So, again I ask, Who are we doing this for? Once we ask the right question, realizing our true identity and purpose, we can read the Proverbs for women with confidence and appreciation.

Be warned, however, Proverbs has scathing words to the ill-tempered and quarrelsome wife, one who destroys her own home, and to the indiscrete woman. These attitudes and behaviors are condemned, giving us opportunity to pause and ask ourselves, does that sound like me?

Proverbs 31 is a particularly intimidating passage for some women, but we will discuss why that is not necessary.

I believe Proverbs brings insight to women (and men) about the importance of character, wisdom, and self-control. *Who can find a virtuous and capable wife? She is more precious than rubies.* Prov 31.10

To Women

- Prov 11.22 *Like a gold ring in a pig's snout is a beautiful woman who shows no discretion.*

- Prov 14.1 *The wise woman builds her house, but with her own hands the foolish one tears hers down.*

- Prov 19.14 *Houses and wealth are inherited from parents, but a prudent wife is from the Lord.*

- Prov 21.9 and 25.24 *Better to live on a corner of the roof, than to share a house with a quarrelsome wife.*

- Prov 21.19 *It's better to live alone in the desert than with a quarrelsome, complaining wife.*[1]

- Prov 27.15-16 *A quarrelsome wife is like a constant dripping on a rainy day; restraining her is like restraining the wind or grasping oil with the hand.*

- Prov 12.4 *A wife of noble character is her husband's crown, but a disgraceful wife is like decay in his bones.*

*****

We are given a remarkable testimony in Proverbs 31.

For many years, I've heard this passage and witnessed countless women interpret it as a list of "to dos" or some kind of definition of a woman's role. How tragic!

It was written by a woman! King Lemuel's mother gave him this poem, written with an acrostic in Hebrew, to guide him in choosing a godly and capable wife. This was not a job description, but a heart description.

When we as women are confused by the ideals of feminism (independence, power, living for self) or the denigration of traditionalism (dependence, subjugation, living for others), we find ourselves viewing the Proverbs 31 woman as a passage of roles, duties, and responsibilities. We feel suffocated and crushed by the weight of such high expectations.

If we are secure in our identity (created by God, bearing his image) and purpose (reflecting aspects of His nature and character, as *ezers*), our lens through which we read Proverbs 31 brings greater clarity and appreciation.

A woman secure in the fact that she was created in His image and fashioned with strength and capacity for aiding and allying begins to see more of herself in the Proverbs 31 woman.

She is secure that her calling is not to live a life serving self or others. Her life is in service to her Creator and is best expressed through her relationships.

To the husband, she is the *ezer kenegdo*: the essential counterpart, his corresponding strength, and of priceless worth to him. That's why Lemuel's mother stressed, *She is worth far more than rubies...Give her the reward she has earned, and let her works bring her praise at the city gates.*[36]

Men, acknowledge and appreciate the strength your godly wives bring to bear in your marriages! Joyfully praise God and her for such gifts!

To the friend, relative, work associate, or her children, she is also an *ezer*, recognizing and filling needs through her insight, strength, and support.

As she lives a life intent on reflecting her maker, she begins to naturally do things for the betterment of others in her life, not out of self-promotion and a desire to control, nor out of duty and obligation, but out of love and devotion to God, whose image she mirrors within the framework of those relationships.

Proverbs 31 then becomes a celebration. It develops into a passage that celebrates the *ezer* strength and the many contexts it is expressed throughout a woman's lifetime.

PROV 31.10-31

10 *A wife of noble character who can find? She is worth far more than rubies.*

11 *Her husband has full confidence in her, and lacks nothing of value.*

12 *She brings him good, not harm, all the days of her life.*

13 *She selects wool and flax and works with eager hands.*

14 *She is like the merchant ships, bringing her food from afar.*

15 *She gets up while it is still dark; she provides food for her family and portions for her servant girls.*

16 *She considers a field and buys it; out of her earnings she plants a vineyard.*

17 *She sets about her work vigorously; her arms are strong for her tasks.*

18 *She sees that her trading is profitable, and her lamp does not go out at night.*

19 *In her hand she holds the distaff and grasps the spindle with her fingers.*

20 *She opens her arms to the poor and extends her hands to the needy.*

21 *When it snows, she has no fear for her household; for all of them are clothed in scarlet.*

22 *She makes coverings for her bed; she is clothed in fine linen and purple.*

23 *Her husband is respected at the city gate, where he takes his seat among the elders of the land.*

24 *She makes linen garments and sells them, and supplies the merchants with sashes.*

25 *She is clothed with strength and dignity; she can laugh at the days to come.*

26 *She speaks with wisdom, and faithful instruction is on her tongue.*

27 *She watches over the affairs of her household and does not eat the bread of idleness.*

28 *Her children arise and call her blessed; her husband also, and he praises her:*

29 *"Many women do noble things, but you surpass them all."*

30 *Charm is deceptive, and beauty is fleeting; but a woman who fears the Lord is to be praised.*

31 *Give her the reward she has earned, and let her works bring her praise at the city gate.*

Appendix

In Genesis we find the Creation story: God created the heavens and the earth, then spoke light into existence; He made the sky, gave form to the land and seas, planted the earth with grass, trees, shrubs, then populated the earth and seas with fish, birds, and land-dwelling animals.

All of creation was teeming with life. He then created a man named Adam, and afterwards, a helper for him, a woman later named Eve. They were created in His image, to rule over His magnificent creation, to *Be fruitful and increase in number; fill the earth and subdue it.* Genesis 1:28

They lived in the Middle East, in Eden where God situated a garden, believed to be located in the Fertile Crescent of modern-day Turkey, Syria, and Iraq.

This garden was a sanctuary of sorts, possibly even a mountain, serving as a temple for worship and fellowship between God and man.

The Garden of Eden wasn't just any garden with pretty foliage and a serene ambiance. This truly was paradise, His paradise. It was the best of everything; after all, God Himself created it!

Every aspect of it was intentionally designed with beauty and artistry. He held nothing back; it was the peak of luxury and extravagance. Adam and Eve lacked for nothing. Their basic needs were simple and fully met in Him.

Personally, I believe that is why people flock to tropical escapes for rest and rejuvenation. Something cries out from within our souls to return to Eden!

*****

Adam and Eve were innocent and naked, tasked with overseeing care of the garden[37] and ruling over all living creatures.

Scripture states that God had not yet sent rain to the earth as streams rose up from the earth and watered the whole surface of the ground. This garden sanctuary had a river actually flowing out of it, which separated into four headwaters.

This prefigures the River of Life in the Holy City, a New Jerusalem, *clear as crystal, flowing from the throne of God and of the Lamb down the middle of the great street of the city,* spoken of in Revelation 22.1-2.

This was an early temple: the place where God and man met, had fellowship, and enjoyed each other's presence.

Everything was perfect and new, and man could only marvel at God's wisdom, love, and power manifested by His creation.

In the middle of the garden, He placed two remarkable trees: the Tree of Life and the Tree of the Knowledge of Good and Evil.

The significance of the Tree of Life escaped me for most of my life, as the focal point on this story was always on the other tree, the Tree of the Knowledge of Good and Evil, where everything went askew.

But we cannot ignore the truth presented in black and white. There was a Tree of Life, intended to sustain life indefinitely and eternally, which was God's provision for his most exalted masterpieces, mankind, the ones He made in His own likeness and image.

It was His plan for us from the very beginning, to live in community with Him forever. God has *set eternity in the hearts of men; yet they cannot fathom what God has done from beginning to end.* Ecclesiastes 3.11

God instructed Adam, *You are free to eat from any tree in the garden; but you must not eat from the Tree of the Knowledge of Good and Evil, for when you eat of it, you will surely die.* Genesis 2.16

This was God's first covenant with mankind. He gave them authority and rule over creation, assigned them to work the garden and increase in number, but He warned that they must never eat from the Tree of the Knowledge of Good and Evil.

*****

God trusted Adam and Eve in His beautiful, perfect creation to do as He said. Yet, we all know how the story goes. Eve, that foolish woman, had a conversation with a serpent that duped her into an earth shattering mistake. It was a life and death decision. Literally.

The Tree of Life promised life eternal, and the Tree of the Knowledge of Good and Evil promised certain death.

Did God really say, "You must not eat from any tree in the garden?" Genesis 3.1

The serpent, Satan, knew that God did not say those exact words, but he was taking Eve down a path in her logic that she should not have traveled.

She answered him, *We may eat fruit from the trees in the garden, but God did say, "You must not eat fruit from the tree that is in the middle of the garden and must not touch it, or you will die."* Genesis 3.2

I feel a bit sorry for Eve right here, because I do wonder if she fully understood the meaning of the word "die." She had not witnessed things, animals, or people dying; that had never happened before. Yet, she was told clearly what to avoid and the consequences it would yield.

However, confusion and doubt were introduced.

You will not surely die, for God knows that when you eat of it your eyes will be opened and you will be like God, knowing good and evil. Genesis 3.5

How conniving! Satan simply suggested that she was missing out, that God was withholding, and there was knowledge she was not privy to.

She saw that the fruit of the tree was good for food and pleasing to the eye, and also desirable for gaining wisdom, she took some and ate it. She also gave some to her husband, who was with her, and he ate it. Genesis 3.6

*****

Why didn't Adam stop her? Why did he not interject himself into the conversation? We don't know. All we know is, *She gave some to her husband who was with her, and he ate it.* Genesis 3.6

Then, something peculiar happened. *The eyes of both of them were opened, and they realized they were naked; so they sewed fig leaves together and made coverings for themselves.* Genesis 3.7-8

For the first time ever, they felt shame.

God had not created them to hide themselves, but the realization of their error brought about a new experience, one that made them shrink back, seeking to conceal what felt exposed and out of sync with every other experience they had known.

John 3.20 states, *Everyone who does evil hates the light, and will not come into the light for fear that his deeds will be exposed.*

They felt naked and ashamed for the first time in their lives. Today, we might say, they were mortified, as that word describes an intense feeling of embarrassment. However, it also means to bring death, or deaden, and that is exactly what happened to their hearts and their bodies.

*****

Later, God arrived to visit them in the garden, and of course, they hid from him.

> *"Where are you?" God called out to the man. Man answered, "I heard you in the garden, and I was afraid because I was naked; so I hid." And he said, "Who told you that you were naked? Have you eaten from the tree that I commanded you not to eat from?" The man said, "The woman you put here with me—she gave me some fruit from the tree, and I ate it." Then the LORD God said to the woman, "What is this you have done?" The woman said, "The serpent deceived me, and I ate."*
> Genesis 3.9b-13

What followed next were the curses from God, not the same cursing man does sinfully but a righteous sentencing of man and creation for breaking their covenant with God.

First, He dealt with the serpent, the instigator, and cursed it to crawl on its belly and to eat dust for the rest of its life. (This actually strikes me as odd, as if the serpent did not already crawl, did it swim or somehow walk?)

Next, he put enmity (ill will, hatred) between the serpent and the woman, between its offspring and hers. Yet, he provided a gracious plan for redemption, *He [the woman's offspring] will crush your head [serpent], and you will strike [at] his heel.* Genesis 3.15

Followers of Christ recognize that there is a battle to be fought and suffering to endure for a while, as we live in a decaying world still vulnerable to and deceived by spiritual forces of evil.

Yet Christ, the particular offspring of woman spoken of in Genesis, would endure suffering and crush the serpent's head in His victory over death.

Immediately God made a new covenant (a formal, binding promise) to redeem mankind from this fall into sin and death!

*****

The next curse God gave was to the woman, that her pains in childbirth would be increased. (Translation: It is entirely possible that you could die giving birth, but if you do not, you certainly will feel like you are dying.)

After increased pain in childbirth, God told Eve that *your desire will be for your husband, and he will rule over you.* Genesis 3.16b

Many interpret this latter phrase to reflect the battle in leadership over households between women and men, the latter of which, God specified to be the true head of the family and home.

Eve would be subject to the leadership and authority of her husband from that point forward.

This prescribed hierarchy accounts for some of the relational issues many deal with in marriages today and in our society as a whole. Man is to lead and protect the woman, but woman desires autonomy and leadership over the man.

*****

To Adam, God gave an even greater judgment and curse:

Because you listened to your wife and ate from the tree about which I commanded you, "You must not eat of it," cursed is the ground because of you; through painful toil you will eat of it all the days of your life. It will produce thorns and thistles for you and you will eat the plants of the field. By the sweat of your brow, you will eat your food, until you return to the ground since from it you were taken; for dust you are and to dust you will return. Genesis 3.17-19

This marked the beginning of man's struggle in work: the need to earn a living and provide for himself and his family. It is a struggle, it makes us sweat, it wears us out. It is work.

But the last sentence revealed a devastating reality: you are going to die.

*****

God warned Adam and Eve that if they ate from the Tree of the Knowledge of Good and Evil, they would die. It was not immediate. Lightning did not strike them the moment they bit into the fruit. But, it was impending.

Death was the eventual physical consequence for their disobedience and one of ultimate finality. Life will end. Your life will cease. *For as dust you are, to dust you will return.* Genesis 3.19

This world and life cannot go on forever, as it has been violated and broken by betrayal.

*****

The final judgment was banishment from paradise:

The man has now become like one of us, knowing good and evil. He must not be allowed to reach out his hand and take also from the tree of life and eat, and live forever. So the LORD God banished him from the Garden of Eden to work the ground from which he had been taken. After he drove the man out, he placed on the east side of the Garden of Eden cherubim and a flaming sword flashing back and forth to guard the way to the Tree of Life. Genesis 3.22-24

This was the most tragic and fatal effect of the fall of man. Being cast out of paradise and separated from God, mankind was relegated to the rest of creation, now injured and dying. Man must navigate life with this new knowledge, this awareness of good and evil, as well as the desires that would come with such knowledge.

Adam and Eve's life went from a perfect, eternal existence in the presence of God to a life of labor, filled with complicated relationships, struggles for survival, impending death, and a necessary separation from the One who never wanted any of this for them.

I often wonder how it must have felt for this couple to be banished from paradise. They had only each other to live out the consequences of their sin. It must have been a lonely new world, already fading in its glory, shattered by the effects of their sin.

Adam and Eve had no friends yet that we know of, no one to share this lonely burden with but each other.

That's what sin does to us. It isolates and brings pain and death.

We see it in broken relationships. We feel it in sickness and diseases. We sense it in our loneliness and separation from God.

A great rift was formed that day in the garden, one that tore through the seams of the physical and spiritual universe. It brought about a chasm so immense that regardless of desire, self-effort, or knowledge, no man could ever span. No one could restore things to their original order.

Except One.

*****

Many people today view God as harsh, dictatorial, distracted, uncaring, lofty, disconnected, and the list goes on and on.

But what most have failed to realize is that WE have made life the difficult struggle that it is today. God did not create the struggle we endure.

God set mankind up in a glorious garden, full of beauty and peace, and only asked one thing in return. Solomon declared in Ecclesiastes 7.29, *God made mankind upright, but men have gone in search of many schemes.*

Adam and Eve did not realize that the cost of their disobedience would forever alter their lives and the lives of their offspring. They may not have understood all that weighed in the balance.

Instead of true life eternal, they chose death and the knowledge of evil. The price was much greater than they could have ever imagined.

In the words of Shakespeare, "what's done, cannot be undone."

*****

We all identify with Adam and Eve as we are their offspring, and therefore, we too are under the curse of the fall. King David wrote, *Surely I was sinful at birth, sinful from the time my mother conceived me.* Psalm 51.5

We too suffer the consequences of their decision to disobey. Their sin is now OUR sin. And it is OUR sin that brought about judgment. It is OUR sin that leaves us naked and exposed, ashamed in His presence.

Adam and Eve recognized their need for coverings for their bodies, yet God in his love and mercy provided a greater covering for their sin. *The LORD God made garments of skin for Adam and his wife and clothed them.* Genesis 3.21

Their own efforts at hiding the shame and guilt, pitiful little fig leaves sewn together, hid very little, but God's provision was a tunic made from animal skin, providing greater coverage (atonement) and even comfort in their shameful condition.

Even then, God showed compassion on Adam and Eve in their degradation.

*****

Praise God that he has provided atonement (covering) for our sins today!

When Christ, that later offspring of woman, came into this world, He lived a perfect life and sacrificed Himself on the cross for our sins, reconciling and restoring fellowship with our Creator. He was the one man capable of bridging the chasm that stands between God and man.

And *by one sacrifice He has made perfect forever those who are being made holy.* Hebrews 10.14

We no longer have to hide from our Maker, living in the shame of our sin. We no longer stand helpless and ashamed at the edge of broken fellowship.

We can receive complete forgiveness and a restored relationship with God. He can make us perfect forever and holy like His Son. God declared through Jeremiah the prophet, *For I will forgive their wickedness and will remember their sins no more.* Jeremiah 31.34c What great news!

If you do not know Christ personally and have never experienced forgiveness of your sins, I invite you to pray to Him here and now.

> Dear God, I know that I have messed things up; I know that I have sinned and fallen short of what you had intended for me. I also believe that you sent your Son Jesus to die for me, to pay the penalty for my sin. I believe that He was raised from the dead demonstrating His power over sin and death. I accept

His sacrifice on my behalf and declare Him Lord of my life. I now stand forgiven and cleansed of my wrongdoing. Thank you for your love and mercy. And it is in Jesus' name I pray, Amen.

*Please contact us at info@crowningwisdom.com, if you have prayed this prayer and accepted Christ as your Savior. We would love to pray for you and offer additional resources to guide you as a follower of Christ!

Acknowledgements

To God the Father, who sent us His Son, Jesus Christ "the power of God and the wisdom of God." Thank you for choosing people the world considers foolish in order to shame those who think they are wise, for choosing people who are powerless to shame those who are powerful, for choosing those despised by the world, those counted as nothing at all, and using us to bring to nothing what the world considers important—so that none of us have any reason to boast of anything but You. I Corinthians 1.27-30 NLT paraphrased

Throughout the course of this project, five painful years of cataloging, organizing, writing, rewriting, stopping and starting, and finally editing this piece, there have been individuals whose support and encouragement I cannot underscore enough.

First and foremost is the jolly gentle giant: my husband, my best friend, and biggest fan. You talked me out of quitting more times than I can recall. I am thankful that you not only urged me to stay the course, but you also walked it with me, every step of the way. Your faith reassures me, your vision inspires me, and your optimism comforts me! I love you more and more each day!

To my parents, Cliff and Wanda Atkins, who blessed me with a godly legacy which I strive to pass on to my own children. Thank you for your love and obedience to God in training us up in the way we should go. And thank you for your unwavering support and for always being there for those much needed pep talks!

To my parents-in-law, Bob and Bonnie Dawson. Thank you for raising a godly son and for setting a wonderful example of love and faithfulness!

To my children, you bring me such great joy! I understand God's love and grace better each day because of you! I pray that as your parents, we will *guide you in the way of wisdom and lead you along straight paths* in accordance to Prov 4.11.

To Bethany Haycox, Carole Leach, and Laura Thompson, thank you for your willingness to read and edit early versions of this book. Your insight and honesty was priceless! Thank you for your godly wisdom and encouragement in spite of my obvious inadequacies for an endeavor such as this!

To Lauren Eberle, the "pro," who generously edited "final" versions of these stories and assured me that I actually am a writer in spite of my doubts, fears, and inexperience. Thank you. Thank you. Thank you!

To the McNeely, Worley, Stopnik, and Thompson families: We thank God for you! Through the good, the bad, and the baffling, you have loved us and been our *brothers (and sisters) born for adversity*. We pray for God's continued blessings and Crowning Wisdom in your lives!

To Myquillin Smith, for She Speaks, and for encouraging me in this massive endeavor and in those still to come!

And to the "kids" from "Breaking the Cycle," you also inspire me and I genuinely hope Matt and I will be like you two when we "grow up!"

Humbly yours,

Tracie A. Dawson

About The Author

Tracie married her high school sweetheart over twenty years ago. She and her husband have three children and reside in the 'burbs of Charlotte, NC.

She is a former social worker, seasonal homeschooling mother, leads a ladies' Bible Study, and is a worship leader at the church where her husband is pastor. She is passionate about vulnerable populations and focuses on the specific needs of victimized women and children in rural regions of Peru.

She is fiercely competitive, compassionate, and admittedly compulsive, but strives to humbly point everyone to the life-changing wisdom through the Scriptures.

Endnotes

[1] The Holy Bible, New Living Translation Carol Stream, Illinois (Tyndale) 1996, 2004, 2007. All # 1 footnotes are from the above translation.
[2] Matthew 5.45
[3] Philippians 4.7
[4] Hebrews 4.12
[5] Job 1.21b
[6] Isaiah 55.9
[7] Romans 5.3b-4
[8] Romans 5.5
[9] I Corinthians 1.24
[10] Matthew 5.28
[11] Numbers 14.18
[12] Job 8.4
[13] Job 18.21
[14] Colossians 3.12-14
[15] Romans 8.21
[16] Mary Frances Bowley, The White Umbrella: Walking with Survivors of Sex Trafficking, (Chicago, Ill: Moody Publishers, 2012) pg 52.
[17] Matthew 18.3
[18] Matthew 18.15
[19] Galatians 6:1
[20] Colossians 3.16
[21] Philippians 2.3-4
[22] Matthew 25.14-30
[23] Genesis 1.28a
[24] Matthew 7.19
[25] John 15.1-8
[26] Mark 11.13-14
[27] Leviticus 25.23
[28] Proverbs 8.22-23
[29] I Kings 3.3a
[30] I Kings 3.5
[31] I Kings 10.6-9
[32] Proverbs 3.13-14
[33] Isaiah 55.1-2
[34] Ezer: Biblical Femininity, Grace Church, Greenville, SC
[35] Genesis 1.27 (NLT)
[36] Proverbs 31.10b, 31
[37] Genesis 2.15

www.ingramcontent.com/pod-product-compliance
Lightning Source LLC
LaVergne TN
LVHW051521070426
835507LV00023B/3234